JOURNEY *to my* FAITH

Family Devotional Series

Helping Parents Develop Their Children's Love for God and for People

VOLUME 4

DAVID IBRAHIM

ANM
publishers

JOURNEY to my FAITH

VOLUME 4

Paperback ISBN: 978-1-946174-09-3

Published by:

ANM
publishers

Advancing Native Missions
P.O. Box 5303
Charlottesville, VA 22905
www.AdvancingNativeMissions.com

Graphic Design by:
Christopher Kirk, GraphicsForSuccess.com

DEDICATION

Firstly, I take a great opportunity to acknowledge our Lord Jesus Christ for using this empty vessel for His glory.

Secondly, I dedicate this book to my father, who was my spiritual hero and a servant of God, Pastor James W. G. (November 29, 1927 - May 26, 2015). Also to my mother Mrs. Parveen A. G. (October 20, 1933 - April 19, 2017) a godly woman, who has a great hand in my upbringing. Both of them were godly couple, who were great inspiration to all their seven children and their spouses, as well as to their twenty one grand-children, eleven great-grand children, and also tens of thousands to whom they served passionately as their humble shepherds for over sixty years.

ACKNOWLEDGEMENT

I take this great opportunity to acknowledge and thank our Lord Jesus Christ for using this broken vessel for His glory.

As John Donne (1572–1631) said, "No man is an island…" It's amazing how, at times, the Lord puts a certain vision in our lives and brings people along the way in order to accomplish it. We, being in the "body of Christ", need one another. I don't have the words to describe my deepest gratitude, for Ms. Faye Boyd, who put in hours and hours to check the script thoroughly on each page. Ms. Boyd, thank you so much for your patience and willingness to make it possible.

I appreciate Ms. Janet Shaffer and Mr. Tommy Meche, Pastor Richard Cohen, and Annlyn Ouzts, who wholeheartedly brought the work to the next level by checking and correcting any typographical inaccuracies. Also I am grateful for Mr. Paulo R. Gill's services in research efforts, and lastly, but most importantly, for my dear wife, our children and other concerned friends, who kept encouraging and sharing new ideas to make this project possible.

CONTENTS

INTRODUCTION

And these words which I command you today shall be in your heart. ⁷*You shall teach them diligently to your children, and shall talk of them when you sit in your house, when you walk by the way, when you lie down, and when you rise up.* ⁸*You shall bind them as a sign on your hand, and they shall be as frontlets between your eyes." (Deuteronomy 6:6-8)*

Why Use the Quotes & My Challenge to You

After the publication of Volume 1 of *Journey to My Faith*, the one question I have been asked most is, "Why have you included quotations from people who are not Christians?" This is a good and valid question because, as believers in Jesus, we should always live and speak what is true and right. This especially is so when God blesses us with children and has given us the responsibility to raise them in a godly manner. So let me explain to you why I have included quotations from people who do not believe in Jesus Christ for salvation.

First, let's talk about where truth comes from. If you were to ask believers where they think truth comes from, most would probably say that it comes from the Bible. However, the Bible has, directly or indirectly, mentioned only some of the truths that have been discovered, but not all of them.

Does that mean those math principles and scientific discoveries are less true than the truth that we learn in the Bible that says there is only one God, or that salvation comes through faith in Jesus Christ alone? It comes down to this. All truth is not mentioned in the Bible, but all truth is from God. More specifically, truth is defined by the character of God because God is truth (Deuteronomy 32:3,4; John 14:6; 15:26; 16:13). Before there was anything material or immaterial, God was. Truth, just like everything else, finds its origin in God Himself. (A more detailed description of this is included in Volume 2.)

You can go through everything that is truth, and it will point back to one or more aspects of God's character because truth is defined by who God is.

The question then remains—are people who do not have their faith in Jesus Christ for salvation and therefore are not made alive in Christ unfit to speak or share truth? Let's look at this more closely. All human beings are made in the image of God, saved or unsaved (Genesis 1:26). The Bible talks about how God has put eternity in each person's heart (Ecclesiastes 3:11). I believe this includes a capability to discern God-defined truth, even in our fallen, sinful state.

Our role as parents is one of discernment. This is true from the start of God blessing us with our children. From the things they watch, see, read, and hear, we should filter the information that is presented to our children. In some cases, that means totally censoring the information. In others, it means turning that into a teachable moment with discussion while we allow the information to be presented.

My encouragement to you as parents is that, when you get to the end of each daily devotion in *Journey to My Faith*, be discerning with the quotes. Use them as discussion points with your kids. Talk with your children about whether what is quoted is truth and look to Scripture to verify it.

The Need

The lessons are focused and based on The Holy Bible, so that the children will learn with understanding the purpose why the Savior came for all mankind. This only could be experienced by knowing God's Word and having a personal relationship with His Son. This is the very heart of Jesus Christ that shall not perish (John 3:16).

Just as children grow physically, they also need spiritual nourishment, on a daily basis, to grow in their faith. Research has concluded that in the early stages of growth, children have the capability to absorb anything taught to them, like a sponge. This leaves a lasting impact on them for the rest of their lives.

We have seen the discipline Muslims parents have, for making sure that the children will go to the Mosque or Madrassa (Islamic school) on a daily basis. The effort behind this is to educate them with the core of Islamic faith, and for the children to memorize the whole Quran. This concept is an honor for the family, and it roots the children firm in their faith, till death. On daily basis, Muslims parents are determined to set aside one or two hours for their children to focus on their religious values and teachings.

In America or Europe, generally children attend public/government schools for 6-7 hours daily, 5 days a week, 10 months each year for the length of 12 years. Christian parents don't always have an option to implement a Christian worldview. Competing worldview is here, and subtle to imprint its on our children. Unfortunately, in our society, 90% of our children are being educated by the very system that is itself the problem. Those forces who have rejected, and have completely eliminated Biblical principals from their schools, now have embraced evolution. Therefore, this is a time of urgency. We need to be on fire for the Lord, and realize that our children are our mission field. We as Christians are not called to "fit in," but to "stand out."

Parents' Responsibility

Since the Lord has blessed us with such a wonderful gift of parenthood, we make sure to do our best to take care of children's physical needs like clothing, schooling and food. However, the question is, who is accountable to fulfill that "Spiritual Gap"? It is our responsibility to fill the void in the lives of our children, who are our Mission field. Many parents have the misconception that it's the responsibility of the "Sunday School" teachers to teach their children about Biblical values and heritage. Just 30-45 minutes a week are not enough for spiritual grooming. Rather, as parents, it's your everyday duty as Scripture commands us:

> *"This Book of the Law shall not depart from your mouth, but you shall meditate in it day and night that you may observe to do according to all that is written in it. For then you will make your way prosperous, and then you will have good success." (Joshua 1:8)*

I am humbled to share that the Lord planted a seed in my heart, to work on a daily Bible study for the families with school-aged children. The vision began when I started traveling back and forth to Pakistan. During that time duration, I met many parents who showed concern for the spiritual growth of their children. Although parents want to guide their children, they are unable to do so thoroughly and systematically, due to the lack of Biblical material that captures children's interest.

The concept of Sunday school, in third world countries, is entirely different from that in the West, where it's mostly organized according to age. However, in developing countries, due to limited space in the church building, children of all ages are accommodated in one room. The lesson is generalized from kindergarten to higher grades, therefore only major Biblical stories are taught repeatedly. The writer's desire is that this workbook will be translated into other major languages, and be circulated as an outreach tool around the world, to indigenous church groups.

Being a parent of growing children myself, this thought truly stirred my heart with a burden: that it's our responsibility to raise our children in the fear of the Lord on a daily basis at home. According to the research done and penned in the book titled *Already Gone*, by Mr. Ken Ham and his co-writers, the shocking survey result was that only 11% of the children after high school return to the church. Where are we as parents failing to do our part? Why do 89% of our children want nothing to do with Christianity anymore? This has puzzled me, and thus, after prayerfully seeking God's wisdom, the Lord gave me the vision that resulted in the birth of this workbook: *Journey to My Faith.*

Methodology

Each lesson is planned, not only to help your children, but also to help you, as a parent, learn about the basic Biblical truths. Also, much time was dedicated to gathering all the general information that makes these lessons interesting. The intention of the writer is not to overwhelm the children, although on some days you will read more than 30 Bible verses, which focus on one thought for that specific day.

End Results

The purpose of this journal is not to merely promote religious facts, but rather the Biblical and Spiritual depth of Christianity. It is a daily Bible study for the whole family, studying from Genesis through Revelation. The children will know, chronologically, the theme, purpose and synopsis of each book of the Bible, along with the number of chapters in each book. Each week, the children will memorize one or two Bible verses expressing the main foundation of our Christian faith. Also, the focus is on the Biblical method of evangelism, which is not based on any denomination or para-church organization, but solely on the foundation of Biblical Truth. Furthermore, reading the amazing stories of great men and women of the Bible, whom God chose, will also broaden children's understanding about who the God of Abraham, Isaac and Jacob really is, and His characteristics and attributes found both in the Old and New Testaments.

Simultaneously, children will increase their general knowledge about each country, learning fascinating facts about different areas, and their global impact. They will learn about inventions, and read quotes of great men and women, who have wholeheartedly contributed to the welfare and improvement of humanity, in the fields of geography, mathematics, medicine, politics, philosophy, science, and technology. Additionally, the short weekly tests and reviews will help you evaluate what your children have studied.

As you assist your children in gaining the spiritual truths through this book, children will realize that God is more than able to use His people mightily for His glory, as long as we allow Him to work in our lives, with humility and submission. I have great confidence that one day, by God's grace, your children's names will be included in the fields of future discoveries and inventions that will benefit humanity. Primarily, though, it is important that they will be soul winners for the Lord in the years to come.

It's my humble prayer that every day, as you go through these pages with your children, the Lord will be the source of your wisdom, strength, joy, and perseverance, revealing the insights of His mysteries and revelations to you. Most importantly, I pray that whatever you do or wherever you go as a family, you will be a sweet fragrance of Christ. Others can sense the Lord's presence and reverence in your life, in all the days to come.

So I close with a quote from Solomon, which personally has touched and transformed my inner being: "The fear of the Lord is the beginning of wisdom; and the knowledge of the holy is understanding." (Proverbs 9:10)

PRAYER GUIDELINES

I hope that you and your children will spend quality time in prayer, by observing Biblical principles, and by giving its ultimate importance in your daily lives.

What is Prayer?

It is communication with God, at anytime. The scriptures give some guidelines of how we are to pray. The Lord's Prayer has the complete pattern for us on how to pray...

> [5] *"And when you pray, you shall not be like the hypocrites. For they love to pray standing in the synagogues and on the corners of the streets, that they may be seen by men. Assuredly, I say to you, they have their reward.* [6] *But you, when you pray, go into your room, and when you have shut your door, pray to your Father who is in the secret place; and your Father who sees in secret will reward you openly.* [7] *And when you pray, do not use vain repetitions as the heathen do. For they think that they will be heard for their many words.* [8] *Therefore do not be like them. For your Father knows the things you have need of before you ask Him." (Matt 6:5-8)*

Ask

Although our Heavenly Father knows the things we need, we still should ask, for James tells us, *"You do not have because you do not ask."* (James 4:2-3) So it is crucial that we should keep asking, seeking and knocking. *"So I say to you, ask, and it will be given to you; seek, and you will find; knock, and it will be opened to you."* (Luke 11:9) *"Casting all your care upon Him, for He cares for you."* (1 Peter 5:7) This should comfort you as you consider the challenges and needs of you and your family. Remember that your spiritual responsibility is to daily bathe your loved ones in prayer, for their future destiny can be preserved by your prayers for them.

Intercede

The word "intercede" means, "to intervene on behalf of another." Hebrews 7:25 tells us that Jesus lives to make intercession for us. He is our Pattern, our Leader, and our Shepherd. If He is interceding for us, then we are surely called to intercede for others. Pray for those who burden your heart, or as the Holy Spirit directs you. While prayer can differ daily, intercession should be the centerpiece of prayer, not only for your family, but also for your friends, neighbors, colleagues, church, pastor, and national leaders, etc., especially for those who are nonbelievers in Jesus Christ. A very important point is that intercessory prayer takes place in the spiritual realm, where the battles are won or lost.

Speak Scriptures

During your prayer, it is very important to speak scripture verses to express that you "have faith in God." There are things we ask of God, but then He sometimes leads us to proclaim or declare things. (Mark 11:21-24) He clearly tells us that we can speak to the mountain under certain conditions and the mountains will be removed. When Satan tempts you to feel lonely, forgotten or even deserted, declare God's Word that assures you of His promise to bless and comfort you during difficult times. In order to do that, you must, *"Study to show thyself approved unto God."* (2 Tim. 2:15)

In your prayers speak God's Word over you, your family members, and friends. Remember those scriptural assurances that *"by His stripes, we are healed"* (Isaiah 53:5), *"All my needs are met according to His riches in glory by Christ Jesus"* (Philippians 4:19), and, most importantly, *"I can do all things through Christ who strengthens me"* (Philippians 4:13).

Repentance

Many of us understand the term "repentance" means "turning from sin." However, the biblical definition of "repent" means "to change one's mind." The Bible also tells us that true repentance will result in a change of actions (Luke 3:8-14; Acts 3:19). So, the full biblical definition of repentance is, a change of mind that results in a change of action. Acts 26:20 declares, *"I preached that they should repent and turn to God and prove their repentance by their deeds. For godly sorrow produces repentance leading to salvation, not to be regretted; but the sorrow of the world produces death."* (2 Corinthians 7:10)

The Lord tells us in Psalm 51:17 that He will not turn away a broken and contrite or repentant heart! He will not turn us away! God's Word clearly says that, if one hides iniquity in his heart, He will not hear him. (Psalm 66:18) So once you give Him thanks, praise and worship, your heart is open to confess your sins. When you've done this, you need to believe by faith that your sins truly are forgiven, and the result will be great inner peace. He not only forgives your sins, He will also enable you to resist leaning toward rebellion and independence, if you ask.

Enjoy His Presence

As you spend great quality time with Jesus, render unto Him praise and thanksgiving, and speak the Word, you will sense Him very near and will enjoy His presence.

During your prayer time, worship, read, meditate, and rejoice in a God who hears you when you call on His name. The scripture clearly assures us through the Words spoken to Jeremiah, *"For I know the thoughts that I think toward you, says the Lord, thoughts of peace and not of evil, to give you a future and a hope.* [12] *Then you will call upon Me and go and pray to Me, and I will listen to you.* [13] *And you will seek Me and find Me, when you search for Me with all your heart."* (Jeremiah 29.11-13)

While or when you focusing on God's provisions, mercies, and goodness He has brought into your life. He will fill you with the joy of His presence. Always have an attitude of praise and thanksgiving in whatever circumstances you experience, so that His grace will sustain you, and to make you victorious through His Cross. It's very important that your opening and closing prayer each day of the study be done with humility and openness of heart, thus this will render your prayer meaningful and genuine.

> *"The Lord bless you, and keep you: the Lord make his face to shine upon you, and be gracious unto you; The Lord lift up his countenance upon you, and give you peace."* (Numbers 6:24)

"Your word is a lamp to my feet and a
light to my path."

Psalm 119:105

Day 1 ~ *Saul's Conversion*

OPENING PRAYER
READ: Acts 9:1-31

Then Saul, still...

1) What happened to Saul while he was on his way to Damascus?_____
_____

2) How long did Saul fast during his blindness?_____
_____

3) What was Saul preaching? How did people react to him after his conversion?_____
_____
_____

Explore God's World

MEMORY VERSES:
Psalm 23:5-6 "You prepare a table before me in the presence of my enemies; You anoint my head with oil; my cup runs over. 6 Surely goodness and mercy shall follow me, all the days of my life; And I will dwell in the house of the Lord forever."

NAMES OF JESUS CHRIST IN THE BOOK OF REVELATION
8) **Witness** (Rev. 3:14 also **"faithful witness"** in Rev.1:5),
9) **The First and the Last** (Rev. 1:17, 1:11; 21:6; 22:13),
10) **Creator** (Rev. 4:11),
11) **Lion of the Tribe of Judah** (Rev. 5:5),
12) **Root of David** (Rev. 5:5),
13) **Son of God** (Rev. 2:18),

For Your Information

FUN FACTS	THE TOP TEN NATIONS OF CELL PHONE USERS	MIRIAM
1. The Berlin Wall was built in 1961. 2. The writers of the Bible include kings, peasants, priests, philosophers, fishermen, poets, scholars, statesmen, a Pharisee, a physician, a tax collector, and an official in Egypt.	1) China 2) India 3) USA 4) Brazil 5) Russia 6) Indonesia 7) Pakistan 8) Japan 9) Nigeria 10) Bangladesh	...was the older sister of Moses and a prophetess of God, speaking His word as He instructed. She had a strong personality in an age when women were not considered leaders. No doubt she supported her brothers Moses and Aaron, during the difficult trek in the desert. At one point in the wilderness, Miriam's desire for personal glory led her to question God, who punished her with leprosy for seven days.

GROUP DISCUSSION AND CLOSING PRAYER

"The harder you work, the luckier you get."
Gary Player

Day 2 ~ The New Gentile Church in Antioch

OPENING PRAYER
READ: Acts 11:1-30

Now the apostles...

1) What was the vision Peter saw in the city of Joppa?_____
_____

2) Where were the disciples first called the Christians and why were they given this title?_____
_____

_____

3) What kind of man was Barnabas? How long did Saul stay with him at Antioch?_____
_____

_____

Explore God's World

MEMORY VERSES:

Psalm 23:5-6 "You prepare a table before me in the presence of my enemies; You anoint my head with oil; my cup runs over. [6] Surely goodness and mercy shall follow me, all the days of my life; And I will dwell in the house of the Lord forever."

NAMES OF JESUS CHRIST IN THE BOOK OF REVELATION
8) **Witness** (Rev. 3:14 also **"faithful witness"** in Rev.1:5),
9) **The First and the Last** (Rev.1:17, 1:11; 21:6; 22:13),
10) **Creator** (Rev. 4:11),
11) **Lion of the Tribe of Judah** (Rev. 5:5),
12) **Root of David** (Rev. 5:5),
13) **Son of God** (Rev. 2:18),

For Your Information

FUN FACTS	THE TOP TEN NATIONS OF CELL PHONE USERS	BALAAM
1. Winston Churchill died in the year 1965 A.D. 2. In 1867, the USA purchased Alaska from Russia. 3. The Bible was written on the continents of Asia, Africa, and Europe.	1) China 2) India 3) USA 4) Brazil 5) Russia 6) Indonesia 7) Pakistan 8) Japan 9) Nigeria 10) Bangladesh	...("devourer," "swallower up," or "glutton") was a pagan seer hired by the evil King Balak, to put a curse on the Israelites as they were entering Moab. However, against his will, he acted as a mouthpiece for God by blessing Israel instead of cursing them. He had encountered Jehovah, but chose false gods of wealth and fame.

GROUP DISCUSSION AND CLOSING PRAYER

"There's only one way to succeed in anything, and that's to give it everything."
Vince Lombard

Day 3 ~ Paul's First Missionary Journey

OPENING PRAYER
READ: Acts 13:1-48
[cross ref. 2nd & 3rd missionary journey 15:32-18:23; and 21:16]

Now in the church...

1) Who was Bar-Jesus and what happened to him? _____
_____

2) Which were the verses Paul (Saul) "quoted" from the Psalm? _____
_____

3) What was the outcome of the "blessing and conflict" which took place in Antioch? _____
_____
_____

Explore God's World

MEMORY VERSES:
Psalm 23:5-6 "You prepare a table before me in the presence of my enemies; You anoint my head with oil; my cup runs over. 6 Surely goodness and mercy shall follow me, all the days of my life; And I will dwell in the house of the Lord forever."

NAMES OF JESUS CHRIST IN THE BOOK OF REVELATION
8) **Witness** (Rev. 3:14 also **"faithful witness"** in Rev.1:5),
9) **The First and the Last** (Rev.1:17, 1:11; 21:6; 22:13),
10) **Creator** (Rev. 4:11),
11) **Lion of the Tribe of Judah** (Rev. 5:5),
12) **Root of David** (Rev. 5:5),
13) **Son of God** (Rev. 2:18),

For Your Information

FUN FACTS
1. B.C. stands for Before Christ.
2. The Bible was written in three languages: The Old Testament was mostly written in Hebrew with a small percentage in Aramaic, while the New Testament was written in Koine (common or everyday language) Greek.

THE TOP TEN NATIONS OF CELL PHONE USERS
1) China 2) India
3) USA 4) Brazil
5) Russia 6) Indonesia
7) Pakistan 8) Japan
9) Nigeria 10) Bangladesh

JOSHUA
…began life in Egypt as a slave and showed tremendous courage as the leader of the Israelites after Moses' death. He was one of two older men (Caleb being the other) allowed to enter the Promised Land because of his trust in God. He was a brilliant military commander and prospered because he relied upon God with every aspect of his life. With one exception, he always consulted God before battle. Sadly, he did not do so when the people of Gibeon entered into a deceptive peace treaty with Israel.

GROUP DISCUSSION AND CLOSING PRAYER

"A house without books is like a room without windows."
Horace Mann

Day 4 ~ Paul's Imprisonment in Jerusalem

OPENING PRAYER
READ: Acts 21:26-36; 22:22-29; and 23:11-22

Then Paul took...

1) How did the people react when Paul was seen in the temple? Of what did they accuse him?_____
_____
_____

2) Why was it important for the centurion to know that Paul was a Roman citizen?_____
_____

3) Why did those forty men take an oath neither to eat nor drink?_____
_____

Explore God's World

MEMORY VERSES:

Psalm 23:5-6 "You prepare a table before me in the presence of my enemies; You anoint my head with oil; my cup runs over. ⁶ Surely goodness and mercy shall follow me, all the days of my life; And I will dwell in the house of the Lord forever."

NAMES OF JESUS CHRIST IN THE BOOK OF REVELATION
8) **Witness** (Rev. 3:14 also **"faithful witness"** in Rev.1:5),
9) **The First and the Last** (Rev.1:17, 1:11; 21:6; 22:13),
10) **Creator** (Rev. 4:11),
11) **Lion of the Tribe of Judah** (Rev. 5:5),
12) **Root of David** (Rev. 5:5),
13) **Son of God** (Rev. 2:18),

For Your Information

FUN FACTS	THE TOP TEN NATIONS OF CELL PHONE USERS	RAHAB
1. The Berlin Wall was built in 1961. 2. The writers of the Bible include kings, peasants, priests, philosophers, fishermen, poets, scholars, statesmen, a Pharisee, a physician, a tax collector, and an official in Egypt.	1) China 2) India 3) USA 4) Brazil 5) Russia 6) Indonesia 7) Pakistan 8) Japan 9) Nigeria 10) Bangladesh	...was one of those unexpected characters in the Bible. Even though she made her living as a prostitute in Jericho, she recognized the true God and took Him for her own before the destruction of her city by Joshua and his men. She was an ancestor of both King David and Jesus Christ. She earned mention in the Faith Hall of Fame (Hebrews 11:31). She was resourceful, loyal to Israel, and faithful to her word.

GROUP DISCUSSION AND CLOSING PRAYER

"A friend is someone who knows all about you and still loves you."
Elbert Hubbard

Day 5 ~ Righteousness Revealed - Gospel

OPENING PRAYER
READ: Romans 1:1-32

Paul, a bondservant...

1) Why did Paul say "I am a debtor," "I am ready," and "I am not ashamed of the gospel"? _____
_____
_____

2) What does Paul mean when he said "The just shall live by faith"? _____
_____

3) How does "God's wrath on unrighteousness" apply to us? _____
_____
_____

Explore God's World

MEMORY VERSES:
Psalm 23:5-6 "You prepare a table before me in the presence of my enemies; You anoint my head with oil; my cup runs over. [6] Surely goodness and mercy shall follow me, all the days of my life; And I will dwell in the house of the Lord forever."

NAMES OF JESUS CHRIST IN THE BOOK OF REVELATION
8) **Witness** (Rev. 3:14 also **"faithful witness"** in Rev.1:5),
9) **The First and the Last** (Rev.1:17, 1:11; 21:6; 22:13),
10) **Creator** (Rev. 4:11),
11) **Lion of the Tribe of Judah** (Rev. 5:5),
12) **Root of David** (Rev. 5:5),
13) **Son of God** (Rev. 2:18),

For Your Information

FUN FACTS	THE TOP TEN NATIONS OF CELL PHONE USERS	DEBORAH
1. Winston Churchill died in the year 1965 A.D. 2. In 1867, the USA purchased Alaska from Russia. 3. The Bible was written on the continents of Asia, Africa, and Europe.	1) China 2) India 3) USA 4) Brazil 5) Russia 6) Indonesia 7) Pakistan 8) Japan 9) Nigeria 10) Bangladesh	...was both a prophetess and wise ruler of Israel, the only woman among the twelve judges, who obeyed God's commands. In a time of crisis, she trusted Jehovah and took steps to defeat King Jabin, Israel's oppressor. She acted with boldness and integrity in her duties, relying only on God, not herself.

GROUP DISCUSSION AND CLOSING PRAYER

"The man who does not read good books has no advantage over the man who can't read them."
Mark Twain

Day 6 ~ God's Judgment

OPENING PRAYER

READ: Romans 2:17-29 and 3:9-31

Indeed you are...

1) Which is most important, the circumcision of the heart or of the flesh/body?_____
_____

2) How do the sins listed in verses 10-18 affect our relationship with Christ?_____
_____

3) What does "for all have sinned and fall short of the glory of God" means to you?_____
_____
_____

Explore God's World

MEMORY VERSES:

Psalm 23:5-6 "You prepare a table before me in the presence of my enemies; You anoint my head with oil; my cup runs over. [6] Surely goodness and mercy shall follow me, all the days of my life; And I will dwell in the house of the Lord forever."

NAMES OF JESUS CHRIST IN THE BOOK OF REVELATION
8) **Witness** (Rev. 3:14 also **"faithful witness"** in Rev.1:5),
9) **The First and the Last** (Rev.1:17, 1:11; 21:6; 22:13),
10) **Creator** (Rev. 4:11),
11) **Lion of the Tribe of Judah** (Rev. 5:5),
12) **Root of David** (Rev. 5:5),
13) **Son of God** (Rev. 2:18),

For Your Information

FUN FACTS	THE TOP TEN NATIONS OF CELL PHONE USERS	BARAK
1. B.C. stands for Before Christ. 2. The Bible was written in three languages: The Old Testament was mostly written in Hebrew with a small percentage in Aramaic, while the New Testament was written in Koine (common or everyday language) Greek.	1) China 2) India 3) USA 4) Brazil 5) Russia 6) Indonesia 7) Pakistan 8) Japan 9) Nigeria 10) Bangladesh	...was another mighty Hebrew warrior who answered the call of God. He defeated the Canaanite oppressor and united the tribes of Israel, commanding them with skill and daring. He is mentioned in the Hall of Faith in Hebrews 11. He recognized that Deborah's authority had been given to her by God, so he obeyed a woman, something rare in ancient times.

GROUP DISCUSSION AND CLOSING PRAYER

"If we couldn't laugh, we would all go insane."
Robert Frost

Day 7 ~ Week in Review

MATCH THE FOLLOWING

_____ a. Rahab	1. Three languages
_____ b. Three continents	2. Before Christ
_____ c. Alaska	3. 1965 A.D.
_____ d. Deborah	4. A prostitute
_____ e. Berlin Wall	5. Asia, Africa, and Europe
_____ f. Barak	6. Bought by Russia
_____ g. Bible	7. 1961
_____ h. Winston Churchill	8. A prophetess and judge
_____ i. B.C.	9. Hebrew warrior

TRUE OR FALSE — Circle T for true or F for false

T or F   Deborah was both an evil prophetess and unwise ruler of Israel.

T or F   Winston Churchill died in the year 1865 A.D.

T or F   The Bible was written in seven languages.

T or F   Balaam ("devourer," "swallower up," or "glutton") was a pagan seer.

T or F   Miriam was the older sister of Moses, she served as a prophetess of God.

T or F   B.C. Stands for Before Christ.

T or F   The Berlin Wall was built in 1968.

T or F   Joshua showed tremendous courage, despite the huge responsibility given to him.

T or F   Rahab made her living running an inn.

LIST THE TEN NATIONS WITH THE MOST CELL PHONE USERS

1. _____   2. _____

3. _____   4. _____

5. _____   6. _____

7. _____   8. _____

9. _____   10. _____

COMPLETE THE FOLLOWING

a. Barak was _____ mighty _____ warriors who _____ the call of _____.

b. Deborah acted with _____ and integrity in her _____, relying only on _____, not herself.

c. The Bible was _____ on three _____: Asia, _____, and _____.

d. Joshua was a _____ military _____ and prospered because he relied _____ God.

e. In _____, the USA purchased _____ from Russia.

f. Miriam had a _____ personality in an age when _____ were not considered _____.

g. Rahab _____ one of those _____ characters in the _____.

h. The _____ of the Bible include kings, peasants, priests, _____, fishermen, poets, scholars, statesmen, a _____, a physician, a tax collector, and an official in _____.

MEMORIZE AND WRITE

Psalm 23:5-6 _____

_____

_____

LIST THE NAMES OF JESUS CHRIST IN THE BOOK OF REVELATION

1. _____   2. _____

3. _____   4. _____

5. _____   6. _____

DRASTICALLY CHANGED LIVES

When Saul came face to face with Jesus Christ, he put his faith in Him. From then on, Saul's (Paul's) life had never been the same. God is in the business of changing lives. Describe the ways God has changed your life.

_____

_____

_____

_____

_____

Saul's Conversion Coloring Activity

Note, you may make copies of this page to color if multiple family members in the same household want to color the illustration. (See photo on page 6.)

Day 8 ~ The Fruit of Righteousness

Therefore, having been...

OPENING PRAYER
READ: Romans 5:1-21

1) Please explain how you will walk in newness of life. _____
_____

2) While we were yet sinners, who died for us and what price He paid for our redemption?_____
_____

3) Why is there death because of Adam and Life in Jesus Christ?_____
_____

Explore God's World

MEMORY VERSES:

Isaiah 6:7-8 And he touched my mouth with it, and said: "Behold, this has touched your lips; your iniquity is taken away, and your sin purged." 8 Also I heard the voice of the Lord, saying: "Whom shall I send, and who will go for Us?" Then I said, "Here am I! Send me."

NAMES OF JESUS CHRIST IN THE BOOK OF REVELATION
14) **The Lamb** (Rev. 5:6),
15) **The Shepherd** (Rev. 7:17),
16) **Christ [Anointed]** (Rev. 12:10),
17) **Faithful and True** (Rev. 19:11),
18) **Word of God** (Rev. 19:13),
19) **King of Kings and Lord of Lords** (Rev. 19:16),
20) **Beginning and End** (Rev. 21:6),
21) **Morning Star** (Rev. 22.16)

For Your Information

FUN FACTS	THE SEVEN LARGEST SUBMARINES	GIDEON
1. Ruth and Esther are the only books in the Bible named for women.	1) Typhoon Class (Russia)	...was a judge and natural leader, who destroyed an altar to the pagan god Baal. He was slow to believe God had chosen him as a leader, but once convinced of God's presence with him, Gideon was a loyal follower who obeyed the Lord's instructions. He united the Israelites against the enemies and through God's power defeated them. Hebrews 11 includes him in the Faith Hall of Fame.
2. Anno Domini (AD/A.D.) means "in the year of our Lord," not "after death."	2) Borei Class (Russia)	
	3) Ohio Class (USA)	
3. More recently, academic writers prefer to use BCE (Before the Common Era) in place of B.C. and CE (Common Era) instead of A.D.	4) Delta Class (Russia)	
	5) Vanguard Class (UK)	
	6) Triomphant Class (France)	
	7) Akula Class (Russia)	

GROUP DISCUSSION AND CLOSING PRAYER

"Sometimes you make the right decision; sometimes you make the decision right."

Dr. Phil McGraw

Day 9 ~ Freedom from Sin's Tyranny

OPENING PRAYER
READ: Romans 6:1-23

What shall we...

1) What does it mean that "Death no longer has dominion over you"? _____
_____
_____

2) How can you become a slave of God rather than a slave of sin? _____
_____

3) Why are the wages of sin death? Explain verse 23 thoroughly. _____
_____

Explore God's World

MEMORY VERSES:

Isaiah 6:7-8 And he touched my mouth with it, and said: "Behold, this has touched your lips; your iniquity is taken away, and your sin purged." 8 Also I heard the voice of the Lord, saying: "Whom shall I send, and who will go for Us?" Then I said, "Here am I! Send me."

NAMES OF JESUS CHRIST IN THE BOOK OF REVELATION
14) **The Lamb** (Rev. 5:6),
15) **The Shepherd** (Rev. 7:17),
16) **Christ [Anointed]** (Rev. 12:10),
17) **Faithful and True** (Rev. 19:11),
18) **Word of God** (Rev. 19:13),
19) **King of Kings and Lord of Lords** (Rev. 19:16),
20) **Beginning and End** (Rev. 21:6),
21) **Morning Star** (Rev. 22.16)

For Your Information

FUN FACTS	THE SEVEN LARGEST SUBMARINES	JEPHTHAH
1. BCE is used in place of B.C., and CE is used in place of A.D. 2. There are different types of Biblical prayers: confession, praise, thanksgiving, petition, intercession, commitment, forgiveness, confidence, and benediction.	1) Typhoon Class (Russia) 2) Borei Class (Russia) 3) Ohio Class (USA) 4) Delta Class (Russia) 5) Vanguard Class (UK) 6) Triomphant Class (France) 7) Akula Class (Russia)	…was a judge, a ruler, a mighty warrior, and a brilliant military strategist in Israel. He attempted to negotiate with the enemy to prevent bloodshed. Men fought for him because he must have been a natural leader. Without considering all the possible consequences, he made a rash, unnecessary vow that affected his daughter and family.

GROUP DISCUSSION AND CLOSING PRAYER

"Be willing to make decisions. That's the most important quality in a good leader."

T. Boone Pickens

Day 10 ~ Freedom from the Law's Condemnation

OPENING PRAYER
READ: Romans 7:1-25

Or do you not...

1) According to Paul, if the husband is dead, what is the woman free from? _____
_____
_____

2) How is the law holy, and how are the commandments holy, just, and good? _____
_____

3) Explain verses 18-19. How do these verses apply to your personal life? _____
_____

Explore God's World

MEMORY VERSES:

Isaiah 6:7-8 And he touched my mouth with it, and said: "Behold, this has touched your lips; your iniquity is taken away, and your sin purged." 8 Also I heard the voice of the Lord, saying: "Whom shall I send, and who will go for Us?" Then I said, "Here am I! Send me."

NAMES OF JESUS CHRIST IN THE BOOK OF REVELATION
14) **The Lamb** (Rev. 5:6),
15) **The Shepherd** (Rev. 7:17),
16) **Christ [Anointed]** (Rev. 12:10),
17) **Faithful and True** (Rev. 19:11),
18) **Word of God** (Rev. 19:13),
19) **King of Kings and Lord of Lords** (Rev. 19:16),
20) **Beginning and End** (Rev. 21:6),
21) **Morning Star** (Rev. 22.16)

For Your Information

FUN FACTS	THE SEVEN LARGEST SUBMARINES	SAMSON
1. It took approximately 120 years for Noah to build the ark. 2. The United Nations University is located in Tokyo, Japan. 3. Milk, in its natural form, has a certain amount of sugar called lactose.	1) Typhoon Class (Russia) 2) Borei Class (Russia) 3) Ohio Class (USA) 4) Delta Class (Russia) 5) Vanguard Class (UK) 6) Triomphant Class (France) 7) Akula Class (Russia)	…was dedicated as a Nazarite from his conception, a holy man who was to honor God with his life. He used his physical strength to fight Israel's enemies and led Israel for 20 years, but became selfish as God placed him in a position of authority. He was a bad example as a leader, who finally realized his mistakes, returned to God, and sacrificed himself in order to destroy the enemy.

GROUP DISCUSSION AND CLOSING PRAYER

"Patience is the inclination to control the racing mind, which wants to jump ahead."

Balroop Singh

Day 11 ~ *Life in the Power of the Holy Spirit*

OPENING PRAYER
READ: Romans 8:1-39

There is therefore...

1) What has made us free from the law of sin and death?_____
_____
_____

2) What is "hope" and how does it bring you unto the knowledge and understanding of Christ?_____
_____

3) How do you understand Paul "Who shall separate us from the love of...?"?_____
_____

Explore God's World

MEMORY VERSES:

Isaiah 6:7-8 And he touched my mouth with it, and said: "Behold, this has touched your lips; your iniquity is taken away, and your sin purged." 8 Also I heard the voice of the Lord, saying: "Whom shall I send, and who will go for Us?" Then I said, "Here am I! Send me."

NAMES OF JESUS CHRIST IN THE BOOK OF REVELATION
14) **The Lamb** (Rev. 5:6),
15) **The Shepherd** (Rev. 7:17),
16) **Christ [Anointed]** (Rev. 12:10),
17) **Faithful and True** (Rev. 19:11),
18) **Word of God** (Rev. 19:13),
19) **King of Kings and Lord of Lords** (Rev. 19:16),
20) **Beginning and End** (Rev. 21:6),
21) **Morning Star** (Rev. 22.16)

For Your Information

FUN FACTS	THE SEVEN LARGEST SUBMARINES	DELILAH
1. Ruth and Esther are the only books in the Bible named for women. 2. Anno Domini (AD/A.D.) means "in the year of our Lord," not "after death." 3. More recently, academic writers prefer to use BCE (Before the Common Era) in place of B.C. and CE (Common Era) instead of A.D.	1) Typhoon Class (Russia) 2) Borei Class (Russia) 3) Ohio Class (USA) 4) Delta Class (Russia) 5) Vanguard Class (UK) 6) Triomphant Class (France) 7) Akula Class (Russia)	...is famously referred to as a treacherous seductress, since, as Samson's lover, she betrayed him to the Philistines. She coaxed from him the secret to his great strength, which was his long hair. Contrary to popular thought, she herself did not cut his hair, but rather called for a man to shave off the seven locks as Samson was asleep "upon her knee."

GROUP DISCUSSION AND CLOSING PRAYER

"Modern Society has turned blind; considering patience as cowardliness."

Srinivas Shenoy

Day 12 ~ The Justice & Cause of God's Rejection

OPENING PRAYER
READ: Romans 9:1-21 and 10:1-12

I tell the truth...

1) Why did Israel as a nation reject Christ, God's purpose, and God's justice? _____
_____
_____

2) What was Paul's heart's desire and prayer to God for all of Israel? _____
_____

3) What do you have to confess in order to be saved? _____
_____

Explore God's World

MEMORY VERSES:

Isaiah 6:7-8 And he touched my mouth with it, and said: "Behold, this has touched your lips; your iniquity is taken away, and your sin purged." 8 Also I heard the voice of the Lord, saying: "Whom shall I send, and who will go for Us?" Then I said, "Here am I! Send me."

NAMES OF JESUS CHRIST IN THE BOOK OF REVELATION
14) **The Lamb** (Rev. 5:6),
15) **The Shepherd** (Rev. 7:17),
16) **Christ [Anointed]** (Rev. 12:10),
17) **Faithful and True** (Rev. 19:11),
18) **Word of God** (Rev. 19:13),
19) **King of Kings and Lord of Lords** (Rev. 19:16),
20) **Beginning and End** (Rev. 21:6),
21) **Morning Star** (Rev. 22:16)

For Your Information

FUN FACTS	THE SEVEN LARGEST SUBMARINES	ABSALOM
1. BCE is used in place of B.C., and CE is used in place of A.D. 2. There are different types of Biblical prayers: confession, praise, thanksgiving, petition, intercession, commitment, forgiveness, confidence, and benediction.	1) Typhoon Class (Russia) 2) Borei Class (Russia) 3) Ohio Class (USA) 4) Delta Class (Russia) 5) Vanguard Class (UK) 6) Triomphant Class (France) 7) Akula Class (Russia)	...the third son of King David, is described as the most handsome man in the kingdom. Absalom revolted against his father. While he was fleeing from David's men, his long curly hair was caught in the thick branches of a large oak tree. As he hung in the tree, some of David's warriors attacked him, and one of them decided to kill the rebellious son.

GROUP DISCUSSION AND CLOSING PRAYER

"You have not failed until you quit trying."
Gordon B. Hinckley

Day 13 ~ God's Love Toward Israel

OPENING PRAYER
READ: Romans 11:1-36

I say then...

1) Does Paul believe that God will cast away Israel? What did he say about himself?_____
_____
_____

2) What you can learn from verses 26 & 27?_____
_____

3) What is God's covenant, especially for Israel?_____
_____

Explore God's World

MEMORY VERSES:

Isaiah 6:7-8 And he touched my mouth with it, and said: "Behold, this has touched your lips; your iniquity is taken away, and your sin purged." 8 Also I heard the voice of the Lord, saying: "Whom shall I send, and who will go for Us?" Then I said, "Here am I! Send me."

NAMES OF JESUS CHRIST IN THE BOOK OF REVELATION
14) **The Lamb** (Rev. 5:6),
15) **The Shepherd** (Rev. 7:17),
16) **Christ [Anointed]** (Rev. 12:10),
17) **Faithful and True** (Rev. 19:11),
18) **Word of God** (Rev. 19:13),
19) **King of Kings and Lord of Lords** (Rev. 19:16),
20) **Beginning and End** (Rev. 21:6),
21) **Morning Star** (Rev. 22.16)

For Your Information

FUN FACTS	THE SEVEN LARGEST SUBMARINES	HANNAH
1. It took approximately 120 years for Noah to build the ark. 2. The United Nations University is located in Tokyo, Japan. 3. Milk, in its natural form, has a certain amount of sugar called lactose.	1) Typhoon Class (Russia) 2) Borei Class (Russia) 3) Ohio Class (USA) 4) Delta Class (Russia) 5) Vanguard Class (UK) 6) Triomphant Class (France) 7) Akula Class (Russia)	…was the mother of Samuel who was the last judge of Israel. Even though God was silent toward her request for a child for many years, she never stopped praying. She had faith that God would bless her with a child, whom she vowed to dedicate to God.

GROUP DISCUSSION AND CLOSING PRAYER

"Success is getting what you want, happiness is wanting what you got."
W.P. Kinsella

Day 14 ~ Week in Review

MEMORIZE AND WRITE

Isaiah 6:7-8 _____

_____

_____

TRUE OR FALSE — Circle T for true or F for false

T or F   Milk in its natural form has a certain amount of sodium.

T or F   Absalom, King David's 5th son, is described as an ugly man in the kingdom.

T or F   Hannah never doubted God's abilities.

T or F   It took approximately 120 years for Moses to build the ark.

T or F   Ruth and Esther are the only books in the Bible with woman's name.

T or F   The United Nations University is located in Seoul, South Korea.

T or F   Delilah has become famous as a symbol of a treacherous seductress.

T or F   Anno Domini does not mean "after death," but rather "in the year of our Lord."

T or F   BCE is used in place of B.C., and CE is used in place of A.D.

LIST THE SEVEN LARGEST SUBMARINES

1. _____   2. _____

3. _____   4. _____

5. _____   6. _____

7. _____

WHAT ARE THE DIFFERENT TYPES OF BIBLICAL PRAYERS?

_____

_____

_____

_____

_____

COMPLETE THE FOLLOWING

a. Samson was _____ as a Nazarite, a _____ who was to honor _____ with his life

b. The _____ Nations _____ is located in _____ , Japan.

c. Hannah had _____ that God would _____ her with a child, whom she _____ to dedicate to God.

d. Jephthah was a _____ , a ruler, a mighty _____ , and a brilliant _____ strategist in _____ .

e. Delilah _____ from him the _____ to his great _____ , which was his long _____ .

f. Ruth and _____ are the only _____ in the Bible named for _____ .

g. Milk in its _____ form has a _____ amount of _____ called Lactose.

MATCH THE FOLLOWING

_____ a. The ark	1. Brilliant military strategist
_____ b. Gideon	2. Before the Common Era
_____ c. United Nations University	3. Books in the Bible
_____ d. Milk	4. In the year of our Lord
_____ e. BCE	5. A judge and natural leader
_____ f. Samson	6. 120 years
_____ g. Ruth and Esther	7. Lactose
_____ h. Anno Domini	8. Tokyo, Japan
_____ i. Jephthah	9. A Nazarite

SO GREAT A SALVATION

In the book of Romans, Paul goes to great lengths to describe how awesome God's goft of salvation is. Pick one or two things Paul says about salvation in Christ and describe how they are in your life.

_____

_____

_____

_____

_____

_____

_____

Bible Word Search

```
R N S W K Y M V D E H O P E N
E B Y S L N Y O C E R T Y S O
J O H O E I O N D E S Z F O I
E R H D R N A W N E Q I V Z T
C E K D T T S N L H E G R X A
T W C T N F I U W E T R K E N
I O S E R S V D O G D A F V M
O P P U E Z O K P E I G E K E
N E I D C M Q Z R M T V E D D
R T S P I R I T A U T H Q I N
A Q X N T C D F Y N J B G D O
P P I E S T I D E X W D G I C
W O B N U O Z Z R P J V X J R
N L P W J R E D E M P T I O N
S E G A W S S E N W E N A E U
```

CONDEMNATION	DEATH	DESIRE
DOMINION	FREEDOM	FRUIT
HOLY	HOPE	JUSTICE
KNOWLEDGE	NEWNESS	POWER
PRAYER	REDEMPTION	REJECTION
REPENTANCE	RIGHTEOUSNESS	SINNER
SPIRIT	WAGES	

Day 15 ~ Righteousness Living - Sacrifice

OPENING PRAYER
READ: Romans 12:1-21

I beseech you...

1) How should we present our bodies to God? _____
_____

2) What are the Spiritual gifts and how should you use them? _____
_____

3) What are the characteristics of a true Christian? _____
_____

Explore God's World

MEMORY VERSES:

Psalm 100:1-3 "Make a joyful shout to the Lord, all you lands! ² Serve the Lord with gladness; come before His presence with singing. ³ Know that the Lord, He is God; it is He who has made us, and not we ourselves; we are His people and the sheep of His pasture."

NAMES OF JESUS CHRIST IN THE BIBLE
1) **Advocate** (1 John 2:1),
2) **Angel of the Lord** (Genesis 16:7),
3) **Anointed One** (Psalm 2:2),
4) **Apostle** (Hebrews 3:1),
5) **Author and Perfecter of our Faith** (Hebrews 12:2),
6) **Bishop of Souls** (1Peter 2:25),
7) **Branch** (Zechariah 3:8)

For Your Information

FUN FACTS	THE TOP TEN UNIVERSITIES OF THE WORLD	SAMUEL
1. The place of worship of Hindus is the Temple. 2. The place of worship of Muslims is the Masjid / Mosque. 3. Before his conversion Apostle Paul was known as Saul of Tarsus	1) California Institute of Technology, CA, 2) Harvard University, MA, 3) University of Oxford, UK 4) Stanford University, CA 5) Massachusetts Institute of Technology (MIT), MA, 6) Princeton University, NJ, 7) University of Cambridge, UK, 8) University of California, CA, 9) University of Chicago, IL, 10) Imperial College, UK	...was an honest and fair judge, dispensing God's law impartially. As a prophet, he exhorted Israel to turn from idolatry and to serve God alone. He loved and obeyed God without question. His integrity prevented him from taking advantage of his authority. His first loyalty was to God, regardless of what the people or king thought of him.

GROUP DISCUSSION AND CLOSING PRAYER

"All your dreams can come true if you have the courage to pursue them."
Walt Disney

Helping Parents Develop Their Children's Love for God and for People   19

Day 16 ~ Righteousness Practiced

OPENING PRAYER

READ: Romans 15:1-13 and 16:1-16

We then who...

1) How do you bear one another's burden through Christ's love? _____
_____

2) Why did Paul mention Gentiles and how are they viewed in the Old Testament? _____
_____

3) How many sisters were mentioned in Chapter 16, and what was their particular role? _____
_____

Explore God's World

MEMORY VERSES:

Psalm 100:1-3 "Make a joyful shout to the Lord, all you lands! [2] Serve the Lord with gladness; come before His presence with singing. [3] Know that the Lord, He is God; it is He who has made us, and not we ourselves; we are His people and the sheep of His pasture."

NAMES OF JESUS CHRIST IN THE BIBLE
1) **Advocate** (1 John 2:1),
2) **Angel of the Lord** (Genesis 16:7),
3) **Anointed One** (Psalm 2:2),
4) **Apostle** (Hebrews 3:1),
5) **Author and Perfecter of our Faith** (Hebrews 12:2),
6) **Bishop of Souls** (1Peter 2:25),
7) **Branch** (Zechariah 3:8)

For Your Information

FUN FACTS	THE TOP TEN UNIVERSITIES OF THE WORLD	SAUL
1. The place of worship of Sikhs is the Gurud-wara. 2. The place of worship of Jews is the Synagogue. 3. Philemon's runaway slave, Onesimus, was saved by the ministry of Paul.	1) California Institute of Technology, CA, 2) Harvard University, MA, 3) University of Oxford, UK 4) Stanford University, CA 5) Massachusetts Institute of Technology (MIT), MA, 6) Princeton University, NJ, 7) University of Cambridge, UK, 8) University of California, CA, 9) University of Chicago, IL, 10) Imperial College, UK	…was Israel's first king, who reigned for 42 years. Early in his reign he was admired and respected by the people. Later he became impulsive, acting unwisely. His jealousy of David drove him to madness, as evidenced by his constant pursuit of and attempts to kill David. More than once King Saul disobeyed God's instructions, thinking he knew better. Thus, the Spirit of the Lord left him.

GROUP DISCUSSION AND CLOSING PRAYER

"Patience is supported & nurtured by a quality of forgiveness."

Allan Lokos

Day 17 ~ Moral & Ethical Disorders in the Life of the Church

OPENING PRAYER
READ: 1st Corinthians 5:1-13 and 6:12-20

It is actually...

1) What was the sin not found even among the Gentiles, but found in the church? _____
_____

2) How can you glorify God in the flesh and in the spirit? _____
_____

3) What does Paul say about the sin of sexual immorality? Who is the temple of the Holy Spirit? ___
_____

Explore God's World

MEMORY VERSES:

Psalm 100:1-3 "Make a joyful shout to the Lord, all you lands! ² Serve the Lord with gladness; come before His presence with singing. ³ Know that the Lord, He is God; it is He who has made us, and not we ourselves; we are His people and the sheep of His pasture."

NAMES OF JESUS CHRIST IN THE BIBLE
1) **Advocate** (1 John 2:1),
2) **Angel of the Lord** (Genesis 16:7),
3) **Anointed One** (Psalm 2:2),
4) **Apostle** (Hebrews 3:1),
5) **Author and Perfecter of our Faith** (Hebrews 12:2),
6) **Bishop of Souls** (1Peter 2:25),
7) **Branch** (Zechariah 3:8)

For Your Information

FUN FACTS	THE TOP TEN UNIVERSITIES OF THE WORLD	DAVID
1. The place of worship of Daoism/Taoism is called the Gong. 2. The place of worship of Zoroastrian or Parsis is the Fire Temple. 3. The Disciples of Jesus Christ were first called Christians in Antioch.	1) California Institute of Technology, CA, 2) Harvard University, MA, 3) University of Oxford, UK 4) Stanford University, CA 5) Massachusetts Institute of Technology (MIT), MA, 6) Princeton University, NJ, 7) University of Cambridge, UK, 8) University of California, CA, 9) University of Chicago, IL, 10) Imperial College, UK	...was a man after God's own heart because of his trust in Him for protection and deep love for Him throughout his entire life. He was loyal and respectful to Saul, despite the king's crazed pursuit of him. After committing adultery with Bathsheba whose pregnancy he failed to cover up, he had her husband, Uriah the Hittite, killed in battle. Willfully violating God's command, King David took a census of the people. Often an absent father, David was lenient with his children, not disciplining them when necessary.

GROUP DISCUSSION AND CLOSING PRAYER

"Life is 10% what happens to me and 90% of how I react to it."

Charles Swindoll

Day 18 ~ Instruction on Marriage

Now concerning the...

OPENING PRAYER
READ: 1st Corinthians 7:1-24

1) What are the basic principles of marriage? _____
_____

2) What are marriage vows and how can one follow them? _____
_____

3) Which commandments of God do believers need to follow?_____
_____

Explore God's World

MEMORY VERSES:

Psalm 100:1-3 "Make a joyful shout to the Lord, all you lands! [2] Serve the Lord with gladness; come before His presence with singing. [3] Know that the Lord, He is God; it is He who has made us, and not we ourselves; we are His people and the sheep of His pasture."

NAMES OF JESUS CHRIST IN THE BIBLE
1) **Advocate** (1 John 2:1),
2) **Angel of the Lord** (Genesis 16:7),
3) **Anointed One** (Psalm 2:2),
4) **Apostle** (Hebrews 3:1),
5) **Author and Perfecter of our Faith** (Hebrews 12:2),
6) **Bishop of Souls** (1 Peter 2:25),
7) **Branch** (Zechariah 3:8)

For Your Information

FUN FACTS	THE TOP TEN UNIVERSITIES OF THE WORLD	JONATHAN
1. The place of worship of Hindus is the Temple. 2. The place of worship of Muslims is the Masjid / Mosque. 3. Before his conversion Apostle Paul was known as Saul of Tarsus	1) California Institute of Technology, CA, 2) Harvard University, MA, 3) University of Oxford, UK 4) Stanford University, CA 5) Massachusetts Institute of Technology (MIT), MA, 6) Princeton University, NJ, 7) University of Cambridge, UK, 8) University of California, CA, 9) University of Chicago, IL, 10) Imperial College, UK	...Saul's son, won an impressive victory over the Philistines at the Pass of Michmash. He was the rightful successor to his father as king. When it became clear that God had rejected his father and that David would become king after Saul's death, Jonathan held no grudge against David, whom he wholeheartedly supported and defended.

GROUP DISCUSSION AND CLOSING PRAYER

"The best time to plant a tree was 20 years ago. The second best time is now."

Chinese Proverbs

Day 19 ~ Instruction on Public Worship & the Lord's Supper

OPENING PRAYER

READ: 1st Corinthians 11:1-31 and 12:12-31

Imitate me, just...

1) How is a woman to behave when she prays or prophesies in the church?_____
_____

2) What is the Lord's Table? Why is it important for us to examine ourselves?_____
_____

3) What is the "more excellent way" Paul showed us to follow?_____
_____

Explore God's World

MEMORY VERSES:

Psalm 100:1-3 "Make a joyful shout to the Lord, all you lands! ² Serve the Lord with gladness; come before His presence with singing. ³ Know that the Lord, He is God; it is He who has made us, and not we ourselves; we are His people and the sheep of His pasture."

NAMES OF JESUS CHRIST IN THE BIBLE
1) **Advocate** (1 John 2:1),
2) **Angel of the Lord** (Genesis 16:7),
3) **Anointed One** (Psalm 2:2),
4) **Apostle** (Hebrews 3:1),
5) **Author and Perfecter of our Faith** (Hebrews 12:2),
6) **Bishop of Souls** (1Peter 2:25),
7) **Branch** (Zechariah 3:8)

For Your Information

FUN FACTS	THE TOP TEN UNIVERSITIES OF THE WORLD	BATHSHEBA
1. The place of worship of Sikhs is the Gurudwara. 2. The place of worship of Jews is the Synagogue. 3. Philemon's runaway slave, Onesimus, was saved by the ministry of Paul.	1) California Institute of Technology, CA, 2) Harvard University, MA, 3) University of Oxford, UK 4) Stanford University, CA 5) Massachusetts Institute of Technology (MIT), MA, 6) Princeton University, NJ, 7) University of Cambridge, UK, 8) University of California, CA, 9) University of Chicago, IL, 10) Imperial College, UK	...was the wife of Uriah, the Hittite, whom David sent to the battle front to ensure his death. (Prophet Nathan confronted David with his sins.) Her first child with David died at an early stage. She bore Solomon and took an oath from David that her son would be the king after him, even though he was not David's first born son, as he had other wives. She was a wise and protective mother but used her position as wife to ensure both her and Solomon's safety when Adonijah, David's son, tried to steal the throne.

GROUP DISCUSSION AND CLOSING PRAYER

"An unexamined life is not worth living."

Socrates

Day 20 ~ *The Greatest Love*

OPENING PRAYER
READ: 1st Corinthians 13:1-13

Though I speak...

1) Which type of love is Paul emphasizing? _____
_____

2) Rejoice not in iniquity, but rejoice in what? _____
_____

3) What are the three things which abide? Which is the greatest of all these?_____
_____

Explore God's World

MEMORY VERSES:

Psalm 100:1-3 "Make a joyful shout to the Lord, all you lands! [2] Serve the Lord with gladness; come before His presence with singing. [3] Know that the Lord, He is God; it is He who has made us, and not we ourselves; we are His people and the sheep of His pasture."

NAMES OF JESUS CHRIST IN THE BIBLE
1) **Advocate** (1 John 2:1),
2) **Angel of the Lord** (Genesis 16:7),
3) **Anointed One** (Psalm 2:2),
4) **Apostle** (Hebrews 3:1),
5) **Author and Perfecter of our Faith** (Hebrews 12:2),
6) **Bishop of Souls** (1Peter 2:25),
7) **Branch** (Zechariah 3:8)

For Your Information

FUN FACTS	THE TOP TEN UNIVERSITIES OF THE WORLD	SOLOMON
1. The place of worship of Daoism/Taoism is called the Gong. 2. The place of worship of Zoroastrian or Parsis is the Fire Temple. 3. The Disciples of Jesus Christ were first called Christians in Antioch.	1) California Institute of Technology, CA, 2) Harvard University, MA, 3) University of Oxford, UK 4) Stanford University, CA 5) Massachusetts Institute of Technology (MIT), MA, 6) Princeton University, NJ, 7) University of Cambridge, UK, 8) University of California, CA, 9) University of Chicago, IL, 10) Imperial College, UK	...was the wisest man who ever lived, but also one of the most foolish. He was a prolific writer, poet, and scientist, plus a builder of a majestic palace, gardens, roads, and government buildings. He built the first temple on Mount Moriah in Jerusalem, a seven-year task that became one of the wonders of the ancient world. Solomon's lust for women (he had many non-Jewish wives and concubines) caused him to stray from God by honoring the pagan gods of his wives. Evidence in Ecclesiastes shows his regret later in life for failing to honor God throughout his reign.

GROUP DISCUSSION AND CLOSING PRAYER

"Education costs money, but then so does ignorance."
Sir Claus Moser

Day 21 ~ Week in Review

MATCH THE FOLLOWING

_____ a. Onesimus
_____ b. Daoism/Taoism
_____ c. Sikhs
_____ d. Hindus
_____ e. Jews
_____ f. Apostle Paul
_____ g. Muslims
_____ h. Zoroastrian or Parsis
_____ i. Samuel

1. The Fire Temple
2. The Synagogues
3. Saul of Tarsus
4. A judge and prophet
5. Philemon
6. Masjid / Mosque
7. The Gurudwara
8. The Temple
9. The Gong

LIST THE NAMES OF JESUS CHRIST IN THE BIBLE

1. _____   2. _____

3. _____   4. _____

5. _____   6. _____

7. _____

TRUE OR FALSE — Circle T for true or F for false

T or F   Jonathan, Saul's son, won a victory over the Philistines by killing Goliath.

T or F   Bathsheba bore Solomon and took an oath from David to be the king after him.

T or F   Prophet Nathan confronted David of his sin.

T or F   Solomon was a prolific writer, poet, scientist, plus built a majestic palace, gardens.

T or F   Eli was an honest and fair judge, dispensing God's law impartially.

T or F   The place of worship of Zoroastrian or Parsis is The Fire Temple.

T or F   The Spirit of God never departed from King Saul.

T or F   David was loyal and respectful to Saul, despite king's crazed pursuit of him.

T or F   The runaway slave of Philemon was Onesimus, who got saved through the ministry of Peter.

MEMORIZE AND WRITE

Psalm 100:1-3 _____

_____

_____

_____

LIST THE TOP TEN UNIVERSITIES OF THE WORLD

1. _____   2. _____

3. _____   4. _____

5. _____   6. _____

7. _____   8. _____

9. _____   10. _____

COMPLETE THE FOLLOWING

a. The place of _____ of Sikhs is called the _____.

b. Saul was _____ first _____, who reigned for _____ years.

c. The disciples of _____ were first called _____ in _____.

d. Bathsheba first _____ with David _____ at an early _____.

e. The place of _____ of Muslims is The _____ / _____.

f. Solomon was the _____ man who ever _____ and also one of the _____ foolish.

g. David was a _____ after God's own _____ because of his _____ in Him for and deep _____ for Him.

h. Before his _____, Apostle Paul was known as _____ of _____.

THE GREATEST OF THESE

The end of the 13th chapter of 1st Corinthians states that love is the greatest. Describe in your own words how love is the greatest in your life.

_____

_____

_____

_____

_____

_____

_____

_____

_____

Note, you may make copies of this page to color if multiple family members in the same household want to color the illustration.

Day 22 ~ The Superiority of Prophecy over Tongues

Pursue love, and...

OPENING PRAYER
READ: 1st Corinthians 14:1-25

1) Why is there a need for tongues to be interpreted in the church?_____
_____
_____

2) Who is greater, the person who speaks in tongues or the person who prophesies?_____
_____

3) Why did Paul say "Let your women keep silent in the churches..."?_____
_____

Explore God's World

MEMORY VERSES:

Psalm 100:4-5 "Enter into His gates with thanksgiving, and into His courts with praise. Be thankful to Him, and bless His name. [5] For the Lord is good; His mercy is everlasting, and His truth endures to all generations."

NAMES OF JESUS CHRIST IN THE BIBLE
8) **Bread of Life** (John 6:35,48),
9) **Bridegroom** (Matthew 9:15),
10) **Carpenter** (Mark 6:3),
11) **Chief Shepherd** (1 Peter 5:4),
12) **The Christ** (Matthew 1:16),
13) **Comforter** (Jeremiah 8:18),
14) **Consolation of Israel** (Luke 2:25),
15) **Chief Cornerstone** (Ephesians 2:20)

For Your Information

FUN FACTS	THE WORLD'S HIGHEST WATER FALLS	ELIJAH
1. Joseph was in slavery for 13 years before he become overseer to the king of Egypt. 2. Fats and carbohydrates are essential parts of our food because they provide energy. 3. The Trans-Siberian Railway (USSR), connecting Moscow to Vladivostok, is the longest railway line in the world.	1) Angel Falls, Venezuela 2) Tugela Falls, South Africa 3) Cataratas las Tres Hermanas, Peru 4) Olo'upena Falls-Molokai, Hawaii, USA 5) Cataratas Yumbilla, Peru 6) Vinnufossen Falls, Norway 7) Puukaoku Falls, Hawaii, USA	...did not die, he was taken up by God to heaven in a chariot. With incredible faith in God, he was an instrument for God's miracles against Israel's idolaters. He struck a heavy blow against the false gods when he challenged the Queen's pagan prophets to a test as whether Baal or the Israelite God is the true God. After the stunning victory on Mount Carmel, he fled for his life because the Queen sought his death for having her prophets killed. Alone, Elijah fell into depression, but the Lord was patient with him, for the prophet had more work to do.

GROUP DISCUSSION AND CLOSING PRAYER

"Build your own dreams, or someone else will hire you to build theirs."

Farrah Gray

Day 23 ~ Seeing the Glory of God with Unveiled Faces

OPENING PRAYER
READ: 2nd Corinthians 3:4-18 and 4:1-15

And we have...

1) What is the difference between the spirit and the letter of the law? _____
_____
_____

2) How would your life be without hope? _____
_____

3) What did Paul preach, which source did he use? _____
_____

Explore God's World

MEMORY VERSES:

Psalm 100:4-5 "Enter into His gates with thanksgiving, and into His courts with praise. Be thankful to Him, and bless His name. [5] For the Lord is good; His mercy is everlasting, and His truth endures to all generations."

NAMES OF JESUS CHRIST IN THE BIBLE
8) **Bread of Life** (John 6:35,48),
9) **Bridegroom** (Matthew 9:15),
10) **Carpenter** (Mark 6:3),
11) **Chief Shepherd** (1 Peter 5:4),
12) **The Christ** (Matthew 1:16),
13) **Comforter** (Jeremiah 8:18),
14) **Consolation of Israel** (Luke 2:25),
15) **Chief Cornerstone** (Ephesians 2:20)

For Your Information

FUN FACTS	THE WORLD'S HIGHEST WATER FALLS	JEZEBEL
1. Canada has the lowest death rate in the world. 2. The dimensions of Noah's ark were at least 135 meters long (300 cubits), 22.5 meters wide (50 cubits), and 13.5 meters high (30 cubits). That's 450 feet long, 75 feet wide, and 45 feet high.	1) Angel Falls, Venezuela 2) Tugela Falls, South Africa 3) Cataratas las Tres Hermanas, Peru 4) Olo'upena Falls-Molokai, Hawaii, USA 5) Cataratas Yumbilla, Peru 6) Vinnufossen Falls, Norway 7) Puukaoku Falls, Hawaii, USA	...influenced her husband king of Israel, to establish Baal worship throughout Israel, thus turning people away from the God who had rescued them from slavery in Egypt. She was clever, but used her intelligence for evil purposes. Because of her persecution and slaughter of God's prophets, plus other evil acts, God's vengeance came through her being thrown from an upper window, then her body was deliberately run over by a soldier's chariot. As prophesied, dogs ate most of her body before she could be buried.

GROUP DISCUSSION AND CLOSING PRAYER

"Dream big and dare to fail."

Norman Vaughan

Day 24 ~ The Ministry of Reconciliation

OPENING PRAYER

READ: 2nd Corinthians 5:1-15 and 6:11-18

For we know...

1) What is the confidence you have through Christ Jesus?_____
_____

2) As a follower of Christ, what must you consider when contemplating your appearance before the Judgment Seat of Christ? _____
_____

3) How can you explain and apply verses 14-16 to your life? _____
_____

Explore God's World

MEMORY VERSES:

Psalm 100:4-5 "Enter into His gates with thanksgiving, and into His courts with praise. Be thankful to Him, and bless His name. [5] For the Lord is good; His mercy is everlasting, and His truth endures to all generations."

NAMES OF JESUS CHRIST IN THE BIBLE
8) **Bread of Life** (John 6:35,48),
9) **Bridegroom** (Matthew 9:15),
10) **Carpenter** (Mark 6:3),
11) **Chief Shepherd** (1 Peter 5:4),
12) **The Christ** (Matthew 1:16),
13) **Comforter** (Jeremiah 8:18),
14) **Consolation of Israel** (Luke 2:25),
15) **Chief Cornerstone** (Ephesians 2:20)

For Your Information

FUN FACTS	THE WORLD'S HIGHEST WATER FALLS	ELISHA
1. Sri Lanka is the largest tea exporting country in the world. 2. The Great Wall of China (1400 mi or 2253 km) is the longest wall in the world. 3. Though Faith, Hope, and Love are very important, the greatest of these is Love.	1) Angel Falls, Venezuela 2) Tugela Falls, South Africa 3) Cataratas las Tres Hermanas, Peru 4) Olo'upena Falls-Molokai, Hawaii, USA 5) Cataratas Yumbilla, Peru 6) Vinnufossen Falls, Norway 7) Puukaoku Falls, Hawaii, USA	...was given a double portion of Elijah's spirit after seeing his mentor taken up to heaven. He was a valuable counselor to kings because of his prophetic insight and wisdom. Like his mentor Elijah, Elisha demanded the people's rejection of idols and their faithfulness to the true God. His miracles, both spectacular and minor, showed that God can change history as well as the everyday lives of his followers. The miracles he performed were many more than that of his predecessor.

GROUP DISCUSSION AND CLOSING PRAYER

"You can't use up creativity. The more you use, the more you have."

Maya Angelou

Day 25 ~ The Collection for the Christians at Jerusalem

OPENING PRAYER
READ: 2nd Corinthians 8:1-15 and 9:6-15

Moreover, brethren, we...

1) Explain what it means by, "that you, through His poverty, might become rich." _____
_____

2) What kind of poverty and riches are Paul talking about: worldly or spiritually? _____
_____

3) Why does God love a cheerful giver? How much should we give back to God? _____
_____

Explore God's World

MEMORY VERSES:

Psalm 100:4-5 "Enter into His gates with thanksgiving, and into His courts with praise. Be thankful to Him, and bless His name. ⁵ For the Lord is good; His mercy is everlasting, and His truth endures to all generations."

NAMES OF JESUS CHRIST IN THE BIBLE
8) **Bread of Life** (John 6:35,48),
9) **Bridegroom** (Matthew 9:15),
10) **Carpenter** (Mark 6:3),
11) **Chief Shepherd** (1 Peter 5:4),
12) **The Christ** (Matthew 1:16),
13) **Comforter** (Jeremiah 8:18),
14) **Consolation of Israel** (Luke 2:25),
15) **Chief Cornerstone** (Ephesians 2:20)

For Your Information

FUN FACTS	THE WORLD'S HIGHEST WATER FALLS	REBELLIOUS SONS
1. Joseph was in slavery for 13 years before he become overseer to the king of Egypt. 2. Fats and carbohydrates are essential parts of our food because they provide energy. 3. The Trans-Siberian Railway (USSR), connecting Moscow to Vladivostok, is the longest railway line in the world.	1) Angel Falls, Venezuela 2) Tugela Falls, South Africa 3) Cataratas las Tres Hermanas, Peru 4) Olo'upena Falls-Molokai, Hawaii, USA 5) Cataratas Yumbilla, Peru 6) Vinnufossen Falls, Norway 7) Puukaoku Falls, Hawaii, USA	...refer to sons, who turned out badly, though they had fathers with godly, honorable positions. The two sons of Aaron, the high priest, offered unsanctioned sacrifices. (Leviticus 10) The two sons of Eli the priest abused their priestly position and were called "worthless men." (1st Samuel 2) Samuel's two sons took bribes and perverted justice. (1st Samuel 8).

GROUP DISCUSSION AND CLOSING PRAYER

"Our lives begin to end the day we become silent about things that matter."
Martin Luther King Jr.

Day 26 ~ Paul's Defense of His Apostolic Authority

Now I, Paul,...

OPENING PRAYER
READ: 2 Corinthians 10:1-17

1) What are the weapons of our warfare? _____
_____
_____

2) Who is Paul's authority? _____
_____

3) Who are not wise? How will you know them? _____
_____

Explore God's World

MEMORY VERSES:
Psalm 100:4-5 "Enter into His gates with thanksgiving, and into His courts with praise. Be thankful to Him, and bless His name. [5] For the Lord is good; His mercy is everlasting, and His truth endures to all generations."

NAMES OF JESUS CHRIST IN THE BIBLE
8) **Bread of Life** (John 6:35,48),
9) **Bridegroom** (Matthew 9:15),
10) **Carpenter** (Mark 6:3),
11) **Chief Shepherd** (1 Peter 5:4),
12) **The Christ** (Matthew 1:16),
13) **Comforter** (Jeremiah 8:18),
14) **Consolation of Israel** (Luke 2:25),
15) **Chief Cornerstone** (Ephesians 2:20)

THE ARMOR OF GOD

For Your Information

FUN FACTS	THE WORLD'S HIGHEST WATER FALLS	TAMAR
1. Canada has the lowest death rate in the world. 2. The dimensions of Noah's ark were at least 135 meters long (300 cubits), 22.5 meters wide (50 cubits), and 13.5 meters high (30 cubits). That's 450 feet long, 75 feet wide, and 45 feet high.	1) Angel Falls, Venezuela 2) Tugela Falls, South Africa 3) Cataratas las Tres Hermanas, Peru 4) Olo'upena Falls-Molokai, Hawaii, USA 5) Cataratas Yumbilla, Peru 6) Vinnufossen Falls, Norway 7) Puukaoku Falls, Hawaii, USA	...was violated by Amnon, her half-brother and David's eldest son. Absalom, who was her real brother, waited two years to avenge his sister's humiliation by sending his servants to murder the drunken Amnon at a feast to which Absalom had invited all the king's sons. Afterwards, Absalom fled to Talmai, king of Geshur.

GROUP DISCUSSION AND CLOSING PRAYER

"Either write something worth reading or do something worth writing."
Benjamin Franklin

Day 27 ~ Defense of the Apostolic Authority of the Gospel Message

OPENING PRAYER
READ: Galatians 1:1-17 and 2:1-10

Paul, an apostle...

1) What made Paul a bondservant of Christ? _____
_____
_____

2) How did Paul explain the revelation of Jesus Christ to the Galatians? _____
_____

3) What desire did James, Cephas, and John have in common with Paul and Barnabas?_____
_____

Explore God's World

MEMORY VERSES:

Psalm 100:4-5 "Enter into His gates with thanksgiving, and into His courts with praise. Be thankful to Him, and bless His name. [5] For the Lord is good; His mercy is everlasting, and His truth endures to all generations."

NAMES OF JESUS CHRIST IN THE BIBLE
8) **Bread of Life** (John 6:35,48),
9) **Bridegroom** (Matthew 9:15),
10) **Carpenter** (Mark 6:3),
11) **Chief Shepherd** (1 Peter 5:4),
12) **The Christ** (Matthew 1:16),
13) **Comforter** (Jeremiah 8:18),
14) **Consolation of Israel** (Luke 2:25),
15) **Chief Cornerstone** (Ephesians 2:20)

For Your Information

FUN FACTS	THE WORLD'S HIGHEST WATER FALLS	METHUSELAH
1. Sri Lanka is the largest tea exporting country in the world. 2. The Great Wall of China (1400 mi or 2253 km) is the longest wall in the world. 3. Though Faith, Hope, and Love are very important, the greatest of these is Love.	1) Angel Falls, Venezuela 2) Tugela Falls, South Africa 3) Cataratas las Tres Hermanas, Peru 4) Olo'upena Falls-Molokai, Hawaii, USA 5) Cataratas Yumbilla, Peru 6) Vinnufossen Falls, Norway 7) Puukaoku Falls, Hawaii, USA	...was the oldest man in the Bible; he lived 969 years. However, he was not unique for his time. Jared lived for 962 years, Noah lived for 950 years, Seth lived for 912 years, Enos lived for 905 years, and Mahalalel lived for 895 years. The first man, Adam, lived for 930 years.

GROUP DISCUSSION AND CLOSING PRAYER

"Change your thoughts and you change your world."
Norman Vincent Peale

Day 28 ~ Week in Review

TRUE OR FALSE — Circle T for true or F for false

T or F   Elisha protected the kings and armies of Israel as did his mentor Elijah.

T or F   Tamar was killed by her brothers Amnon and Absalom.

T or F   Jezebel was clever but used her intelligence for wrong purposes.

T or F   Sri Lanka is the largest corn exporting country in the world.

T or F   Joseph was in slavery for 33 years before he became overseer.

T or F   After a stunning victory on Mount Carmel, Elijah was very happy and successful.

T or F   The Trans-Siberian Railway (USSR) connects Moscow to Vladivostok.

T or F   The Great Wall of China (1400 mi or 2253 km) is the longest wall in the world.

T or F   Samuel's two sons took bribes and perverted justice (1st Samuel 8).

T or F   Elijah died a natural death when he was in the temple

LIST THE SEVEN HIGHEST WATERFALLS

1. _____   2. _____

3. _____   4. _____

5. _____   6. _____

7. _____

COMPLETE THE FOLLOWING

a. Though Faith, _____, and Love are very important, the _____ of these is _____.

b. Elijah did not _____; he was _____ up by God to _____ in a chariot.

c. Canada has the _____ death _____ in the _____.

d. The _____ Elisha performed were _____ more than that of his _____.

e. Tamar was _____ by Amnon her half- _____ and _____ eldest _____.

f. Fats and _____ are an _____ part of our _____ because they _____ energy.

g. Joseph was in _____ for 13 _____ before he become _____ to the _____ of Egypt.

h. As prophesied, _____ ate most of Jezebel's _____ before she could be _____.

MEMORIZE AND WRITE

Psalm 100:4-5 _____

_____

_____

MATCH THE FOLLOWING

_____ a. Great Wall of China   1. 969 years

_____ b. Tamar   2. Baal

_____ c. Elijah   3. Longest Railway line

_____ d. Canada   4. 13 years slavery

_____ e. Jezebel   5. Lowest death rate

_____ f. Trans-Siberian Railway   6. Amnon

_____ g. Joseph   7. 1400 mi or 2253 km

_____ h. Methuselah   8. Mount Carmel

WRITE THE NAMES OF JESUS CHRIST IN THE BIBLE

1. _____   2. _____

3. _____   4. _____

5. _____   6. _____

7. _____   8. _____

CHEERFULLY GIVE

Being happing is giving seems like a paradox. Our world has a hard time thinking that losing something of value can bring happiness or joy. Just as God has joy in giving freely to us so must we have joy as we freely give. Write down any examples from your life that this has happened. If there is none, examine and write down how giving can bring joy just as it brings God joy as He gives.

_____

_____

_____

_____

_____

_____

The Armor of God Coloring Activity (Label Each of the Armor Pieces)

Note, you may make copies of this page to color if multiple family members in the same household want to color the illustration.

Day 29 ~ *Justification of the Gospel Message*

O foolish Galatians!...

OPENING PRAYER

READ: Galatians 3:1-29 and 4:21-31

1) How does Paul, in the book of Galatians, address the theme of justification by faith?_____
_____
_____

2) Who are now Abraham's seed? _____
_____

3) What are two covenants which Paul mentions?_____
_____

Explore God's World

MEMORY VERSES:

Matthew 5:3-4 "Blessed are the poor in spirit, for theirs is the kingdom of heaven. ⁴ Blessed are those who mourn, for they shall be comforted."

NAMES OF JESUS CHRIST IN THE BIBLE
16) **Dayspring** (Luke 1:78),
17) **Day Star** (2 Peter 1:19),
18) **Deliverer** (Romans 11:26),
19) **Desire of Nations** (Haggai 2:7),
20) **Emmanuel** (Matthew 1:23),
21) **Everlasting Father** (Isaiah 9:6),
22) **First Fruits** (1 Corinthians 15:23),
23) **Foundation** (Isaiah 28:16)

For Your Information

FUN FACTS	SEVEN COUNTRIES WITH THE MOST INTERNET USAGE	THE MOST WIVES
1. The Japanese call their country Nippon. 2. Moses was in the wilderness for 40 years, working as a shepherd, before God called him back to Egypt to deliver his people.	1) Iceland 2) Norway 3) Sweden 4) Denmark 5) Netherlands 6) Luxembourg 7) Finland	...Solomon had the most recorded wives in the Bible: 300 princess wives and 700 concubines (female slaves). Many of his marriages were political alliances through daughters of foreign kings in exchange for promises of peace.

GROUP DISCUSSION AND CLOSING PRAYER

"When everything seems to be going against you, remember that the airplane takes off against the wind, not with it."

Henry Ford

Day 30 ~ Practical Implications of the Gospel Message

You ran well...

OPENING PRAYER

READ: Galatians 5:7-25 and 6:1-15

1) In one word tell how the law was fulfilled?_____

2) What are the works of the flesh and the fruit of the Spirit?_____

_____

_____

_____

3) Why is it important for you to bear another's burdens, be generous, and do good to others?_____

_____

_____

Explore God's World

MEMORY VERSES:

Matthew 5:3-4
"Blessed are the poor in spirit, for theirs is the kingdom of heaven. [4] Blessed are those who mourn, for they shall be comforted."

NAMES OF JESUS CHRIST IN THE BIBLE
16) **Dayspring** (Luke 1:78),
17) **Day Star** (2 Peter 1:19),
18) **Deliverer** (Romans 11:26),
19) **Desire of Nations** (Haggai 2:7),
20) **Emmanuel** (Matthew 1:23),
21) **Everlasting Father** (Isaiah 9:6),
22) **First Fruits** (1 Corinthians 15:23),
23) **Foundation** (Isaiah 28:16)

For Your Information

FUN FACTS	SEVEN COUNTRIES WITH THE MOST INTERNET USAGE	GOLIATH OF GATH
1. Verkoyansk in Siberia is the coldest place on the earth. 2. The length of the English Channel is 350 mi or 564 km 3. The two books of the Bible that do not mention God are Esther and the Song of Solomon.	1) Iceland 2) Norway 3) Sweden 4) Denmark 5) Netherlands 6) Luxembourg 7) Finland	...was the Bible's tallest man. He was a Philistine giant warrior who measured "six cubits and a span," or about 9 1/2 feet tall, with 24 fingers and toes, 6 on each hand and 6 on each foot. He was beheaded with his own sword by the young David Bar-Jesse, who single-handedly killed the giant with a stone from a sling shot. While King Saul was also tall, his height is given as being "head and shoulders above everyone else."

GROUP DISCUSSION AND CLOSING PRAYER

"Remember no one can make you feel inferior, without your consent."
Eleanor Roosevelt

Day 31 ~ *Salvation by God's Grace Alone*

OPENING PRAYER
READ: Ephesians 2:1-22

Paul, an apostle...

1) What is God's gift to you? _____

2) Who are the uncircumcision and how are they brought near by the blood of Christ? _____

3) How do you explain Christ as our peace and our cornerstone? _____

Explore God's World
MEMORY VERSES:
 Matthew 5:3-4 "Blessed are the poor in spirit, for theirs is the kingdom of heaven. ⁴ Blessed are those who mourn, for they shall be comforted."

NAMES OF JESUS CHRIST IN THE BIBLE
16) **Dayspring** (Luke 1:78),
17) **Day Star** (2 Peter 1:19),
18) **Deliverer** (Romans 11:26),
19) **Desire of Nations** (Haggai 2:7),
20) **Emmanuel** (Matthew 1:23),
21) **Everlasting Father** (Isaiah 9:6),
22) **First Fruits** (1 Corinthians 15:23),
23) **Foundation** (Isaiah 28:16)

For Your Information

FUN FACTS	SEVEN COUNTRIES WITH THE MOST INTERNET USAGE	DANIEL
1. Trans-Canada is the longest highway in the world (4,860 mi or 7,821 km). 2. The largest quantities of fish in the world are produced by Japan and Russia. 3. Ruth and Rahab are the two gentile women mentioned in the lineage of Jesus	1) Iceland 2) Norway 3) Sweden 4) Denmark 5) Netherlands 6) Luxembourg 7) Finland	...became a skilled officer of the Babylonian king. Excelling at whatever tasks assigned to him, he was first and foremost a servant of God, a prophet who set an example to God's people on how to live a holy life. He survived the lion's den because of his faith in God. As a youth hostage groomed to serve the king, Daniel adapted well to the foreign environment of his captors while keeping his ancestral faith and integrity. God gifted him with visions and interpretation of dreams.

GROUP DISCUSSION AND CLOSING PRAYER

"You may be disappointed if you fail, but you are doomed if you don't try."
Beverly Sills

Day 32 ~ The Mystery of Christ's Body & Our Responsibilities in Him

OPENING PRAYER
READ: Ephesians 3:1-22 and 4:1-4

For this reason I,...

1) What kind of mystery and revelation is Paul talking about? _____
_____

2) Why understand the "Mystery which was hidden in GOD from the beginning of the world"? _____
_____

3) What is the importance of spiritual gifts? Explain briefly "speaking the truth in love." _____
_____

Explore God's World

MEMORY VERSES:

Matthew 5:3-4 "Blessed are the poor in spirit, for theirs is the kingdom of heaven. ⁴ Blessed are those who mourn, for they shall be comforted."

NAMES OF JESUS CHRIST IN THE BIBLE
16) **Dayspring** (Luke 1:78),
17) **Day Star** (2 Peter 1:19),
18) **Deliverer** (Romans 11:26),
19) **Desire of Nations** (Haggai 2:7),
20) **Emmanuel** (Matthew 1:23),
21) **Everlasting Father** (Isaiah 9:6),
22) **First Fruits** (1 Corinthians 15:23),
23) **Foundation** (Isaiah 28:16)

For Your Information

FUN FACTS	SEVEN COUNTRIES WITH THE MOST INTERNET USAGE	NEBUCHADNEZZAR
1. The Japanese call their country Nippon. 2. Moses was in the wilderness for 40 years, working as a shepherd, before God called him back to Egypt to deliver his people.	1) Iceland 2) Norway 3) Sweden 4) Denmark 5) Netherlands 6) Luxembourg 7) Finland	…was a successful conqueror and builder. He defeated Egypt, expanded the Babylonian empire, and lived to be 84 years old. He followed two wise policies: He allowed conquered nations to retain their own religion, and he imported the most intelligent of the conquered peoples to help him govern. At times he recognized Jehovah, but his fidelity was short-lived. Thousands of bricks have been found in Iraq with his name stamped on them.

GROUP DISCUSSION AND CLOSING PRAYER

"Success doesn't come to you, you go to it."
Marva Collins

Day 33 ~ Be Imitators of God & unto Man

OPENING PRAYER

READ: Ephesians 5:1-33 and 6:1-4

Therefore be imitators...

1) How can you walk in the light and wisdom?_____
_____
_____

2) How does the Bible explain the roles of a husband and a wife?_____
_____
_____

3) Which commandment comes with the promise? What are fathers supposed to do?_____
_____

Explore God's World

MEMORY VERSES:

Matthew 5:3-4 "Blessed are the poor in spirit, for theirs is the kingdom of heaven. ⁴ Blessed are those who mourn, for they shall be comforted."

NAMES OF JESUS CHRIST IN THE BIBLE
16) **Dayspring** (Luke 1:78),
17) **Day Star** (2 Peter 1:19),
18) **Deliverer** (Romans 11:26),
19) **Desire of Nations** (Haggai 2:7),
20) **Emmanuel** (Matthew 1:23),
21) **Everlasting Father** (Isaiah 9:6),
22) **First Fruits** (1 Corinthians 15:23),
23) **Foundation** (Isaiah 28:16)

For Your Information

FUN FACTS	SEVEN COUNTRIES WITH THE MOST INTERNET USAGE	JONAH
1. Verkoyansk in Siberia is the coldest place on the earth. 2. The length of the English Channel is 350 mi or 564 km 3. The two books of the Bible that do not mention God are Esther and the Song of Solomon.	1) Iceland 2) Norway 3) Sweden 4) Denmark 5) Netherlands 6) Luxembourg 7) Finland	...was the reluctant prophet who finally recognized the power of God, when he was swallowed by a whale, in whose belly he remained for three days. Jonah had the good sense to repent and thank God for his life. He delivered God's message to Nineveh with skill and accuracy. Jonah mistakenly thought he could run away from God, and thought he knew better than God when it came to the fate of the Ninevites.

GROUP DISCUSSION AND CLOSING PRAYER

"The worst form of inequality is to try to make unequal things equal."

Aristotle

Day 34 ~ Living a Life Worthy with a Servant Attitude for Christ

OPENING PRAYER
READ: Philippians
1:12-26 and 2:1-11

But I want...

1) How are you supposed to preach the Gospel?_____
_____
_____

2) How do you define "For to me, to live is Christ, and to die is gain"?_____
_____
_____

3) To what extent did Christ become obedient and to whom was He obedient?_____
_____

Explore God's World

MEMORY VERSES:

Matthew 5:3-4 "Blessed are the poor in spirit, for theirs is the kingdom of heaven. [4] Blessed are those who mourn, for they shall be comforted."

NAMES OF JESUS CHRIST IN THE BIBLE
16) **Dayspring** (Luke 1:78),
17) **Day Star** (2 Peter 1:19),
18) **Deliverer** (Romans 11:26),
19) **Desire of Nations** (Haggai 2:7),
20) **Emmanuel** (Matthew 1:23),
21) **Everlasting Father** (Isaiah 9:6),
22) **First Fruits** (1 Corinthians 15:23),
23) **Foundation** (Isaiah 28:16)

For Your Information

FUN FACTS	SEVEN COUNTRIES WITH THE MOST INTERNET USAGE	JOSEPH OF NAZARETH
1. Trans-Canada is the longest highway in the world (4,860 mi or 7,821 km). 2. The largest quantities of fish in the world are produced by Japan and Russia. 3. Ruth and Rahab are the two gentile women mentioned in the lineage of Jesus	1) Iceland 2) Norway 3) Sweden 4) Denmark 5) Netherlands 6) Luxembourg 7) Finland	...was the husband of Mary and Jesus' earthly (but not biological) father, who was entrusted by God to raise the Son of God. A skilled carpenter, Joseph believed the angel's explanation for Mary's pregnancy and, in obedience to God, made her his wife instead of quietly "putting her away." The Bible describes him as a righteous man.

GROUP DISCUSSION AND CLOSING PRAYER

"If you want your children to turn out well, spend twice as much time with them, and half as much money."

Abigail Van Buren

42   JOURNEY to my FAITH Family Devotional Series — VOLUME 4

Day 35 ~ Week in Review

MATCH THE FOLLOWING

_____ a. No mention of God   1. Longest highway

_____ b. Ruth and Rahab   2. 350 mi or 564 km

_____ c. Solomon   3. 9 1/2 feet tall

_____ d. Verkoyansk   4. Nippon

_____ e. Trans-Canada   5. Esther and Songs of Solomon

_____ f. Moses   6. Whale

_____ g. English Channel   7. Two gentile women in Jesus' genealogy

_____ h. Japanese   8. 300 wives and 700 concubines

_____ i. Jonah   9. Coldest place

_____ j. Goliath of Gath   10. 40 years

TRUE OR FALSE — Circle T for true or F for false

T or F   Daniel survived the wolves den because of his own strength.

T or F   The length of the English Channel is 850 mi or 564 km.

T or F   Pharaoh had 24 fingers and toes, 6 on each hand and 6 on each foot.

T or F   The Japanese call their country Nippon.

T or F   The largest quantities of fish in the world are produced by Japan and Russia.

T or F   Solomon had only one wife which was selected by his mother.

T or F   Trans-Canada is the third longest highway in the world (4,860 mi or 7,821 km).

T or F   Verkoyansk in Siberia is the hottest place on the earth.

T or F   Nebuchadnezzar was a successful poet and gold digger.

T or F   Jonah was the only prophet who immediately followed God's calling at once.

LIST COUNTRIES WITH THE MOST INTERNET USAGE

1. _____   2. _____

3. _____   4. _____

5. _____   6. _____

7. _____

FILL IN THE BLANKS

a. The _____ of the English _____ is _____ mi or _____ km.

b. _____ in Siberia is the _____ place on the _____.

c. Thousands of _____ have been found in _____ with Nebuchadnezzar's _____ stamped on them.

d. The largest _____ of fish in the world are produced by _____ and _____.

e. The _____ call their _____ Nippon.

f. Trans-_____ is the longest _____ in the _____ (4,860 mi or _____ km).

g. The ____ books of the _____ that do not _____ God are Esther and _____.

h. Ruth and _____ are the _____ gentile women mentioned in the _____ of Jesus.

i. Goliath was a giant _____ who measured "_____ and a span," or about _____ feet ___.

MEMORIZE AND WRITE

Matthew 5:3-4 _____

_____

_____

_____

LIST THE NAMES OF JESUS CHRIST IN THE BIBLE

1. _____   2. _____

3. _____   4. _____

5. _____   6. _____

7. _____   8. _____

THE DISCIPLINE OF GOD

What kinds of things did Israel do that brought the discipline of God on them? In the midst of their time of discipline, had God ever stop loving or caring for them?

_____

_____

_____

_____

Bible Word Search

```
G O N I Q F F W H C M I S J M
R H O M I B U T F Y S N U J J
A G I I A L I L S I A S X N L
C V T T B A S T F I T O K V E
E I A A F Y E T T I F H V D P
U U L T X R T A F N L R C R S
C N E O Y L L I T I W L U A O
E O V R K A C I S N G C E I G
V F E S G A U Y X O A A D D T
O W R K T A B V R Y R V B W W
L E S I M O R P P M J E R E M
Y W O R K S E C A E P I N E J
R N E F Q J S T M F X E Q E S
E N O T S R E N R O C D Q C G
X C O V E N A N T S F Y O N R
```

CORNERSTONE	COVENANTS	FAITH
FRUIT	FULFILLED	GALATIANS
GENEROSITY	GIFTS	GOSPEL
GRACE	IMITATORS	JUSTIFICATION
LOVE	MYSTERY	PEACE
PROMISE	REVELATION	SERVANT
WORKS		

Day 36 ~ Example and Excellence in Commitment

Beware of dogs,...

1) What do you know about Paul's background? _____
_____

2) Who are the enemies of the cross of Christ, and what are their characteristics? _____
_____

3) Whose names are in the Book of Life, and what is to be known to all men? _____
_____
_____

Explore God's World

MEMORY VERSES:

Matthew 5:5-6 "Blessed are the meek, for they shall inherit the earth. [6] Blessed are those who hunger and thirst for righteousness, for they shall be filled."

NAMES OF JESUS CHRIST IN THE BIBLE
24) **Fountain** (Zechariah 13:1),
25) **Friend of Sinners** (Matthew 11:19),
26) **Gate for the Sheep** (John 10:7),
27) **Gift of God** (2 Corinthians 9:15),
28) **God** (John 1:1),
29) **Glory of God** (Isaiah 60:1),
30) **Good Shepherd** (John 10:11),
31) **Governor** (Matthew 2:6)

For Your Information

FUN FACTS	THE TOP TEN TOURIST DESTINATIONS IN THE WORLD	MARY
1. Brazil is famous for football/soccer and the Samba dance. 2. Christianos is from the Greek word meaning "follower of Christ". Christos means "anointed one."	1) France 2) USA 3) China 4) Spain 5) Italy 6) Turkey 7) Germany 8) United Kingdom 9) Russia 10) Malaysia	…was the mother of the Jesus Christ, the Savior of the world. She was a willing servant who trusted God and obeyed His call wholeheartedly. The angel told her that she was highly favored by God; that is, she had been given much grace, or "unmerited favor", from God.

GROUP DISCUSSION AND CLOSING PRAYER

"It is not what you do for your children, but what you have taught them to do for themselves, that will make them successful human beings."

Ann Landers

Day 37 ~ The Supremacy of Christ & Paul's Labor for the Church

READ: Colossians 1:1-23 and 2:1-10

Paul, an apostle of...

1) How does Paul describe the superiority of Christ?_____
_____

2) What does verse 20 mean to you?_____
_____

3) Which is superior: philosophy or Christ? Why?_____
_____
_____

Explore God's World

MEMORY VERSES:

Matthew 5:5-6 "Blessed are the meek, for they shall inherit the earth. [6] Blessed are those who hunger and thirst for righteousness, for they shall be filled."

NAMES OF JESUS CHRIST IN THE BIBLE
24) **Fountain** (Zechariah 13:1),
25) **Friend of Sinners** (Matthew 11:19),
26) **Gate for the Sheep** (John 10:7),
27) **Gift of God** (2 Corinthians 9:15),
28) **God** (John 1:1),
29) **Glory of God** (Isaiah 60:1),
30) **Good Shepherd** (John 10:11),
31) **Governor** (Matthew 2:6)

For Your Information

FUN FACTS	THE TOP TEN TOURIST DESTINATIONS IN THE WORLD	CAESAR AUGUSTUS
1. Greenland is the biggest island of the world. 2. June 5th is observed as World Environment Day. 2. Joshua is a rendering of the Hebrew language "Yehoshua," meaning "Yahweh is salvation."	1) France 2) USA 3) China 4) Spain 5) Italy 6) Turkey 7) Germany 8) United Kingdom 9) Russia 10) Malaysia	…was the first emperor in the ancient Roman Empire, and reigned when Jesus was born. Luke tells us that he ordered a census of the entire Roman world, possibly for tax purposes. He worshiped the pagan Roman gods, but even worse, he regarded himself as a god to be worshipped. The Romans did not invent crucifixion, but they used it extensively to terrorize their subjects.

GROUP DISCUSSION AND CLOSING PRAYER

"A truly rich man is one whom children run into his arms when his hands are empty."

Unknown

Helping Parents Develop Their Children's Love for God and for People

47

Day 38 ~ The Golden Rules for Holy Living

OPENING PRAYER
READ: Colossians 3:5-23 and 4:1-8

Therefore put to...

1) List the things that cause "the wrath of GOD comes upon the sons of disobedience". _____
_____
_____

2) What is the characteristic of a Christian home/family? _____
_____

3) What purpose did Paul mention of Grace and "season with salt" and to whom did he refer?_____
_____
_____

Explore God's World

MEMORY VERSES:

Matthew 5:5-6 "Blessed are the meek, for they shall inherit the earth. ⁶ Blessed are those who hunger and thirst for righteousness, for they shall be filled."

NAMES OF JESUS CHRIST IN THE BIBLE
24) **Fountain** (Zechariah 13:1),
25) **Friend of Sinners** (Matthew 11:19),
26) **Gate for the Sheep** (John 10:7),
27) **Gift of God** (2 Corinthians 9:15),
28) **God** (John 1:1),
29) **Glory of God** (Isaiah 60:1),
30) **Good Shepherd** (John 10:11),
31) **Governor** (Matthew 2:6)

For Your Information

FUN FACTS	THE TOP TEN TOURIST DESTINATIONS IN THE WORLD	THE THREE KINGS
1. The Samaritan woman was the first Gentile evangelist. 2. Grand Central Terminal (New York) is the biggest railway station in the world with its 47 platforms on 48 acres.	1) France 2) USA 3) China 4) Spain 5) Italy 6) Turkey 7) Germany 8) United Kingdom 9) Russia 10) Malaysia	...also known as the Magi, are mentioned only in Matthew. When they discovered that the Messiah was to be born, they organized an expedition to find Him by following a star that led them to Bethlehem. Despite their different culture, beliefs, and birth place, they accepted Jesus as their Savior. Scholars have speculated that they came from Persia, Arabia, or even India.

GROUP DISCUSSION AND CLOSING PRAYER

"I would rather die of passion than of boredom."

Vincent Van Gogh

Day 39 ~ Paul's Defense and Prayer for Spiritual Growth

OPENING PRAYER
READ: 1st Thessalonians 1:2-10; 2:4-9; and 3:1-8

We give thanks...

1) Explain that the Gospel "did not come to you in Word only." _____
_____

2) What did Paul mean when he said that he came as a genuine "Apostle of Christ"?_____
_____

3) Who was Timothy, and for what purpose did Paul send him to Thessalonica?_____
_____
_____

Explore God's World

MEMORY VERSES:

Matthew 5:5-6 "Blessed are the meek, for they shall inherit the earth. [6] Blessed are those who hunger and thirst for righteousness, for they shall be filled."

NAMES OF JESUS CHRIST IN THE BIBLE
24) **Fountain** (Zechariah 13:1),
25) **Friend of Sinners** (Matthew 11:19),
26) **Gate for the Sheep** (John 10:7),
27) **Gift of God** (2 Corinthians 9:15),
28) **God** (John 1:1),
29) **Glory of God** (Isaiah 60:1),
30) **Good Shepherd** (John 10:11),
31) **Governor** (Matthew 2:6)

For Your Information

FUN FACTS	THE TOP TEN TOURIST DESTINATIONS IN THE WORLD	HEROD
1. Brazil is famous for football/soccer and the Samba dance. 2. Christianos is from the Greek word meaning "follower of Christ". Christos means "anointed one."	1) France 2) USA 3) China 4) Spain 5) Italy 6) Turkey 7) Germany 8) United Kingdom 9) Russia 10) Malaysia	…had worked well with Roman conquerors, and was a skilled politician, but also a brutal man who killed his father-in-law, several of his wives, and two of his sons. When the Magi came to look for the Messiah, he slaughtered all the boys under two years old. He ignored the laws of God to suit himself, and chose the favor of Rome over his own people. He was an "Edomite" king over the Jewish people.

GROUP DISCUSSION AND CLOSING PRAYER

"At his best, man is the noblest of all animals; separated from law and justice he is the worst.."

Aristotle

Day 40 ~ Paul's Exhortations to the Thessalonians

OPENING PRAYER
READ: 1st Thessalonians 4:3-18 and 5:12-22

For this is the...

1) On whose authority had Paul taught the Thessalonians how they should live as Christians? _____
_____

2) What is "the Will of God" for every born again Christian? _____
_____

3) What does Paul urge the Christians to do (verses 16-22)?_____
_____
_____

Explore God's World

MEMORY VERSES:

Matthew 5:5-6 "Blessed are the meek, for they shall inherit the earth. ⁶ Blessed are those who hunger and thirst for righteousness, for they shall be filled."

NAMES OF JESUS CHRIST IN THE BIBLE
24) **Fountain** (Zechariah 13:1),
25) **Friend of Sinners** (Matthew 11:19),
26) **Gate for the Sheep** (John 10:7),
27) **Gift of God** (2 Corinthians 9:15),
28) **God** (John 1:1),
29) **Glory of God** (Isaiah 60:1),
30) **Good Shepherd** (John 10:11),
31) **Governor** (Matthew 2:6)

For Your Information

FUN FACTS	THE TOP TEN TOURIST DESTINATIONS IN THE WORLD	ZECHARIAH
1. Greenland is the biggest island of the world.	1) France 2) USA	…the father of John the Baptist, was a holy and upright man, and a priest in the temple. He obeyed God, as the angel had instructed him to raise John as a Nazarite. However, initially, when the angel told Zechariah that his prayer for a child would be answered, the aged priest doubted God's Word.
2. June 5th is observed as World Environment Day.	3) China 4) Spain 5) Italy 6) Turkey 7) Germany	
2. Joshua is a rendering of the Hebrew language "Yehoshua," meaning "Yahweh is salvation."	8) United Kingdom 9) Russia 10) Malaysia	

GROUP DISCUSSION AND CLOSING PRAYER

"A person who never made a mistake never tried anything new."
Albert Einstein

Day 41 ~ Instruction and Injunctions

OPENING PRAYER
READ: 2nd Thessalonians 2:1-15 and 3:1-12

Now, brethren, concerning...

1) Why and to whom did Paul say "not to be soon shaken in mind or troubled,..."? _____

_____

2) Explain "salvation through sanctification by the Spirit." _____

_____

3) Reword 3:8-9. What is the lesson is for you to learn?_____

_____

_____

Explore God's World

MEMORY VERSES:

Matthew 5:5-6 "Blessed are the meek, for they shall inherit the earth. [6] Blessed are those who hunger and thirst for righteousness, for they shall be filled."

NAMES OF JESUS CHRIST IN THE BIBLE
24) **Fountain** (Zechariah 13:1),
25) **Friend of Sinners** (Matthew 11:19),
26) **Gate for the Sheep** (John 10:7),
27) **Gift of God** (2 Corinthians 9:15),
28) **God** (John 1:1),
29) **Glory of God** (Isaiah 60:1),
30) **Good Shepherd** (John 10:11),
31) **Governor** (Matthew 2:6)

For Your Information

FUN FACTS	THE TOP TEN TOURIST DESTINATIONS IN THE WORLD	ELIZABETH
1. The Samaritan woman was the first Gentile evangelist. 2. Grand Central Terminal (New York) is the biggest railway station in the world with its 47 platforms on 48 acres.	1) France 2) USA 3) China 4) Spain 5) Italy 6) Turkey 7) Germany 8) United Kingdom 9) Russia 10) Malaysia	...was the mother of John the Baptist. Elizabeth was sad, but never became bitter because of her barrenness. Her enormous faith in God her entire life resulted from valuing God's mercy and kindness. She praised God for giving her a son. Even though she played a key role in God's plan of salvation, she remained humble by keeping her focus always on the Lord, never on herself.

GROUP DISCUSSION AND CLOSING PRAYER

"Limitations live only in our minds, but if we use our imaginations, our possibilities become limitless."

Jamie Paolinetti

Day 42 ~ Week in Review

LIST THE TOP TEN TOURIST DESTINATIONS IN THE WORLD

1. _____   2. _____
3. _____   4. _____
5. _____   6. _____
7. _____   8. _____
9. _____   10. _____

TRUE OR FALSE — Circle T for true or F for false

T or F   Joshua is a rendering of the Hebrew language "Yehoshua," meaning "Yahweh is salvation."

T or F   The Midianite woman was the first Gentile evangelist.

T or F   Brazil is also famous for football/soccer and the Samba dance.

T or F   Greenland is the smallest island of the world.

T or F   July 25th is observed as World Environment Day.

T or F   Mary trusted God and obeyed His call, but had a few doubts.

T or F   Luke tells us that Caesar Augustus ordered a census taken of the entire Roman world.

T or F   Christianos is from the Arabic word meaning "follower of Christ."

T or F   Herod was a kind man who loved his father-in-law, several of his wives, and sons.

MATCH THE FOLLOWING

_____ a. Grand Central Terminal   1. Yahweh is Salvation

_____ b. Zechariah   2. Jesus Christ

_____ c. Brazil   3. June 5th

_____ d. Mary   4. 1st gentile evangelist

_____ e. Elizabeth   5. Biggest island

_____ f. Christianos   6. Biggest railway station

_____ g. Samaritan woman   7. Soccer and Samba Dance

_____ h. World Environment Day   8. Doubted God's Word

_____ i. Greenland   9. Follower of Christ

_____ j. Yehoshua   10. John the Baptist

FILL IN THE BLANKS

a. The Samaritan _____ was the _____ Gentile _____.

b. _____ Augustus was the 1st _____ in the ancient Roman _____.

c. Christianos is_____ the _____ word meaning "_____ of Christ".

d. June_____ is observed as _____ Environment _____.

e. Mary was the _____ of the _____, the _____ of the world.

f. Brazil is _____ for football/ _____ and the _____ dance.

g. Joshua is a_____ of the _____ language "_____", meaning "Yahweh is _____."

h. Greenland is the _____ island of the _____.

i. Scholars have _____ that the Magi came from _____, Arabia, or even _____.

MEMORIZE AND WRITE

Matthew 5:5-6 _____

_____

_____

_____

DEALING WITH A NEW AND GRWOING CHURCH

As the Apostle Paul went around preaching the gospel, many were getting saved and starting churched. Paul found himself answering many questions of young believers and dealing with issues that came about. Paul knew how to handle each question and issue but answers did not come from himself. What did Paul rely on to give the correct advice? How can you prepare yourself went you need to help someone with questions or issues they face?

_____

_____

_____

_____

_____

_____

_____

_____

Paul Preaches the Gospel Coloring Activity

*Note, you may make copies of this page to color if multiple family members in
the same household want to color the illustration.*

Day 43 ~ Reminders and Regulations in Ministry

OPENING PRAYER
READ: 1st Timothy 1:8-20 and 2:8-15

But we know...

1) How can the Law be good, and what does the Law represent in the Old Testament?_____
_____
_____

2) How does Paul describe Timothy?_____
_____
_____

3) In what circumstances should a "woman learn in silence with all submission"?_____
_____
_____

Explore God's World

MEMORY VERSES:
Matthew 5:7-8 "Blessed are the merciful, for they shall obtain mercy. [8] Blessed are the pure in heart, for they shall see God."

NAMES OF JESUS CHRIST IN THE BIBLE
32) **Great Shepherd** (Hebrews 13:20),
33) **Guide** (Psalm 48:14),
34) **Head of the Church** (Colossians 1:18),
35) **High Priest** (Hebrews 3:1),
36) **Holy One of Israel** (Isaiah 41:14),
37) **Horn of Salvation** (Luke 1:69),
38) **I Am** (Exodus 3:14),
39) **Jehovah** (Psalm 83:18),
40) **Jesus** (Matthew 1:21)

For Your Information

FUN FACTS	THE TOP FIVE COUNTRIES WITH THE BEST EDUCATION SYSTEMS	JOHN THE BAPTIST
1. The Gurkhas are the original inhabitants of Nepal. 2. Babylon was situated on the Euphrates River, about 50 miles south of modern Baghdad, the capital of Iraq.	1) Finland 2) South Korea 3) Hong Kong 4) Japan 5) Singapore	…was six months older than Jesus Christ, his cousin, and the prophesied forerunner of Jesus. His remarkable ministry included the baptism of Jesus in the Jordan River. He lived in the desert wilderness and ate locusts and wild honey. His clothing was made of camel's hair, and he wore a leather belt around his waist. He was put in prison for condemning the immoral marriage of Herod to his brother's wife, Herodias, who schemed to have Herod behead John.

GROUP DISCUSSION AND CLOSING PRAYER

"The worst form of inequality is to try to make unequal things equal."

Aristotle

Day 44 ~ *Qualifications and Responsibilities in Ministry*

OPENING PRAYER

READ: 1st Timothy 3:1-13 and 4:1-11

This is a faithful...

1) List the moral characteristics of a bishop._____
_____

2) What reputation must a deacon have? _____
_____

3) What is the great apostasy Paul foretells 4:1...?_____
_____

Explore God's World

MEMORY VERSES:
Matthew 5:7-8 "Blessed are the merciful, for they shall obtain mercy. [8] Blessed are the pure in heart, for they shall see God."

NAMES OF JESUS CHRIST IN THE BIBLE
32) **Great Shepherd** (Hebrews 13:20),
33) **Guide** (Psalm 48:14),
34) **Head of the Church** (Colossians 1:18),
35) **High Priest** (Hebrews 3:1),
36) **Holy One of Israel** (Isaiah 41:14),
37) **Horn of Salvation** (Luke 1:69),
38) **I Am** (Exodus 3:14),
39) **Jehovah** (Psalm 83:18),
40) **Jesus** (Matthew 1:21)

For Your Information

FUN FACTS
1. Mount Everest was named after Sir George Everest.
2. Peking, China was once called the "Forbidden City."
3. Jesus' first miracle was changing water into wine at the wedding in Cana.

THE TOP FIVE COUNTRIES WITH THE BEST EDUCATION SYSTEMS
1) Finland
2) South Korea
3) Hong Kong
4) Japan
5) Singapore

LAZARUS
...as well as his sisters Mary and Martha were three of Jesus' few friends. He is mentioned by name in the Gospels. When Jesus finally arrived at Bethany after being told of his friend's death, Lazarus had been dead and in his tomb four days. After ordering that the stone over the entrance be rolled away, Jesus raised Lazarus from the dead.

GROUP DISCUSSION AND CLOSING PRAYER

"Challenges are what make life interesting and overcoming them is what makes life meaningful."

Joshua J. Marine

Day 45 ~ Qualifications and Responsibilities in Ministry 2

OPENING PRAYER

READ: 1st Timothy 5:3-20 and 6:6-19

Honor widows who...

1) How are widows to be taken care by the church family?_____
_____

2) How must a Man of God live?_____
_____

3) What are instructions for the rich?_____
_____

Explore God's World

MEMORY VERSES:

Matthew 5:7-8 "Blessed are the merciful, for they shall obtain mercy. [8] Blessed are the pure in heart, for they shall see God."

NAMES OF JESUS CHRIST IN THE BIBLE
32) **Great Shepherd** (Hebrews 13:20),
33) **Guide** (Psalm 48:14),
34) **Head of the Church** (Colossians 1:18),
35) **High Priest** (Hebrews 3:1),
36) **Holy One of Israel** (Isaiah 41:14),
37) **Horn of Salvation** (Luke 1:69),
38) **I Am** (Exodus 3:14),
39) **Jehovah** (Psalm 83:18),
40) **Jesus** (Matthew 1:21)

For Your Information

FUN FACTS
1. The first Governor General of Pakistan was Muhammad Ali Jinnah.
2. Pakistan is the second largest Islamic country in the world, after Indonesia.
3. It took 7 years for the Temple of the Lord to be built by Solomon. (1st Kings 6:38).

THE TOP FIVE COUNTRIES WITH THE BEST EDUCATION SYSTEMS
1) Finland
2) South Korea
3) Hong Kong
4) Japan
5) Singapore

MARTHA AND MARY
...Mary sat at Jesus' feet and listened to His Words. Martha, meanwhile, was distracted and complained about the lack of help with the preparation and serving of the meal. He answered and said to her, "Martha, Martha, you are worried and troubled about many things. But one thing is needed, and Mary has chosen that good part, which will not be taken away from her."

GROUP DISCUSSION AND CLOSING PRAYER

"Too many of us are not living our dreams because we are living our fears."

Les Brown

Day 46 ~ Encouragement and Example in Ministry

I thank God,...

OPENING PRAYER

READ: 2nd Timothy 1:3-14 and 2:1-10

1) Who were Timothy's grandmother and mother and how did Paul regard them? _____

_____

2) What kind of testimony is Paul talking about to Timothy? _____

_____

3) Who is the Seed of David? _____

_____

_____

Explore God's World

MEMORY VERSES:

Matthew 5:7-8 "Blessed are the merciful, for they shall obtain mercy. 8 Blessed are the pure in heart, for they shall see God."

NAMES OF JESUS CHRIST IN THE BIBLE
32) **Great Shepherd** (Hebrews 13:20),
33) **Guide** (Psalm 48:14),
34) **Head of the Church** (Colossians 1:18),
35) **High Priest** (Hebrews 3:1),
36) **Holy One of Israel** (Isaiah 41:14),
37) **Horn of Salvation** (Luke 1:69),
38) **I Am** (Exodus 3:14),
39) **Jehovah** (Psalm 83:18),
40) **Jesus** (Matthew 1:21)

For Your Information

FUN FACTS	THE TOP FIVE COUNTRIES WITH THE BEST EDUCATION SYSTEMS	ZACCHAEUS
1. The Gurkhas are the original inhabitants of Nepal. 2. Babylon was situated on the Euphrates River, about 50 miles south of modern Baghdad, the capital of Iraq.	1) Finland 2) South Korea 3) Hong Kong 4) Japan 5) Singapore	...was a despised chief tax collector for the Roman Empire in Jericho. As Jesus was passing through the region, the short tax collector, desiring to see this man from Galilee, ran ahead and climbed a sycamore tree for a clear view. Jesus looked up and told him to come down because he would stay at his house. Zacchaeus' repentance was evident by his paying back double to those whom he had cheated. Ironically, his name means "pure" or "innocent" in Hebrew. He is considered the shortest man in the Bible.

GROUP DISCUSSION AND CLOSING PRAYER

"You can't fall if you don't climb. But there's no joy in living your whole life on the ground."

Unknown

Day 47 ~ Exhortations in Ministry

OPENING PRAYER
READ: 2nd Timothy 3:1-17 and 4:1-8

But mark this...

1) What will be the "signs of the times" in the last days? _____

_____

2) What did Paul say about the authority of the Scriptures? _____

_____

3) Why did Paul say "I have finished the race and kept the faith"? _____

_____

_____

Explore God's World

MEMORY VERSES:

Matthew 5:7-8 "Blessed are the merciful, for they shall obtain mercy. [8] Blessed are the pure in heart, for they shall see God."

NAMES OF JESUS CHRIST IN THE BIBLE
32) **Great Shepherd** (Hebrews 13:20),
33) **Guide** (Psalm 48:14),
34) **Head of the Church** (Colossians 1:18),
35) **High Priest** (Hebrews 3:1),
36) **Holy One of Israel** (Isaiah 41:14),
37) **Horn of Salvation** (Luke 1:69),
38) **I Am** (Exodus 3:14),
39) **Jehovah** (Psalm 83:18),
40) **Jesus** (Matthew 1:21)

For Your Information

FUN FACTS	THE TOP FIVE COUNTRIES WITH THE BEST EDUCATION SYSTEMS	PETER
1. Mount Everest was named after Sir George Everest. 2. Peking, China was once called the "Forbidden City." 3. Jesus' first miracle was changing water into wine at the wedding in Cana.	1) Finland 2) South Korea 3) Hong Kong 4) Japan 5) Singapore	...was originally called Simon until Jesus renamed him Cephas, an Aramaic word meaning "rock;" in Greek rock means "petros". He remained with Jesus for three years. His faith enabled him to walk on the water for a brief moment. During Jesus' final hours, he not only abandoned Jesus, but denied three times that he even knew Him. However, after Jesus' ascension, Peter became a prominent leader in the early Christian church.

GROUP DISCUSSION AND CLOSING PRAYER

"Life is not measured by the number of breaths we take,
but by the moments that take our breath away."

Maya Angelou

Day 48 ~ God's Grace Displayed within the Church & all Humanity

OPENING PRAYER
READ: Titus 2:1-15 and 3:1-8

You, however,...

1) What is "the sound doctrine"? _____
_____

2) Why should the servant be obedient to his master? _____
_____

3) What was our behavior before "the kindness and love of God our Savior appeared"? _____
_____
_____

Explore God's World

MEMORY VERSES:
Matthew 5:7-8 "Blessed are the merciful, for they shall obtain mercy. [8] Blessed are the pure in heart, for they shall see God."

NAMES OF JESUS CHRIST IN THE BIBLE
32) **Great Shepherd** (Hebrews 13:20),
33) **Guide** (Psalm 48:14),
34) **Head of the Church** (Colossians 1:18),
35) **High Priest** (Hebrews 3:1),
36) **Holy One of Israel** (Isaiah 41:14),
37) **Horn of Salvation** (Luke 1:69),
38) **I Am** (Exodus 3:14),
39) **Jehovah** (Psalm 83:18),
40) **Jesus** (Matthew 1:21)

For Your Information

FUN FACTS	THE TOP FIVE COUNTRIES WITH THE BEST EDUCATION SYSTEMS	ANDREW
1. The first Governor General of Pakistan was Muhammad Ali Jinnah. 2. Pakistan is the second largest Islamic country in the world, after Indonesia. 3. It took 7 years for the Temple of the Lord to be built by Solomon. (1st Kings 6:38).	1) Finland 2) South Korea 3) Hong Kong 4) Japan 5) Singapore	...whose name means "manly," was one of Jesus' disciples and the brother of Simon Peter. Though he doubted, he nevertheless took the boy with two fish and five barley loaves to Jesus, who then multiplied them to feed 5,000. After Acts 1:13 he is never mentioned again. It is not recorded in the Bible, but church tradition says Andrew was crucified as a martyr on a Crux Decussata, that is an X-shaped cross

GROUP DISCUSSION AND CLOSING PRAYER

"When I let go of what I am, I become what I might be."

Lao Tzu

Day 49 ~ Week in Review

LIST THE TOP FIVE COUNTRIES WITH THE BEST EDUCATION SYSTEMS

1. _____ 2. _____

3. _____ 4. _____

5. _____

TRUE OR FALSE — Circle T for true or F for false

T or F   Mary, sat at Jesus' feet and "drank" in His Words.

T or F   Jesus' 11th miracle was changing water into milk at the wedding in Cana.

T or F   Pakistan is the second largest Islamic country in the world, after Indonesia.

T or F   Timothy lived in the desert wilderness and ate locust and wild honey.

T or F   John the Baptist was a chief tax collector for the Roman Empire in Jericho.

T or F   The Gurkhas are the original inhabitants of Nepal.

T or F   It took 17 years to build the Temple of the Lord built by David.

T or F   Babylon was situated on the Euphrates River, about 50 miles south of modern Baghdad.

T or F   Peking, China, was once called the "Forbidden City."

T or F   Mount Alps was named after Sir George Everest.

MATCH THE FOLLOWING

_____ a. Mount Everest   1. Forbidden City

_____ b. Pakistan   2. Ate locusts and wild honey

_____ c. Babylon   3. 7 years

_____ d. Jesus' 1st miracle   4. Pure or innocent

_____ e. The Gurkhas   5. Rock "Petros"

_____ f. The Temple   6. 2nd largest Islamic country

_____ g. Peter   7. Sir George Everest

_____ h. Zacchaeus   8. Nepal

_____ i. John the Baptist   9. Wedding in Cana

_____ j. Peking   10. Baghdad

MEMORIZE AND WRITE

Matthew 5:7-8 _____

_____

_____

FILL IN THE BLANKS

a. _____ is the second _____ Islamic _____ in the _____, after Indonesia.

b. Mount_____ was named after Sir _____ _____.

c. Peter's _____ enabled him to _____ on the _____ for brief moments.

d. Lazarus as _____ as his sisters _____ and _____ were three of _____ few friends.

e. The_____ are the original _____ of Nepal.

f. John the _____, remarkable ministry_____ the baptism of_____ in the _____ River.

g. Jesus' first_____ was _____ water into _____ at the _____ in _____.

h. It took ____years to _____ the _____ of the_____ built by Solomon.

i. Zacchaeus was a _____ chief tax _____ for the _____ Empire in _____.

WRITE AND MEMORIZE THE NAMES OF JESUS CHRIST IN THE BIBLE

1. _____   2. _____

3. _____   4. _____

5. _____   6. _____

7. _____   8. _____

9. _____

HAVING A MENTOR, BEING A MENTOR

The Apostle Paul invested his life into many people and they would go on to do God's work. It is important to invest in the lives of others like Paul did with Timothy and Titus. But it is also important to have mentors in your life to invest into you. Make a list of people who you could be/are mentoring and another list of people who could be/are mentoring you.

_____

_____

_____

_____

Bible Word Search

```
G O N I Q F F W H C M I S J M
R H O M I B U T F Y S N U J J
A G I I A L I L S I A S X N L
C V T T B A S T F I T O K V E
E I A A F Y E T T I F H V D P
U U L T X R T A F N L R C R S
C N E O Y L L I T I W L U A O
E O V R K A C I S N G C E I G
V F E S G A U Y X O A A D D T
O W R K T A B V R Y R V B W W
L E S I M O R P P M J E R E M
Y W O R K S E C A E P I N E J
R N E F Q J S T M F X E Q E S
E N O T S R E N R O C D Q C G
X C O V E N A N T S F Y O N R
```

CORNERSTONE	COVENANTS	FAITH
FRUIT	FULFILLED	GALATIANS
GENEROSITY	GIFTS	GOSPEL
GRACE	IMITATORS	JUSTIFICATION
LOVE	MYSTERY	PEACE
PROMISE	REVELATION	SERVANT
WORKS		

Day 50 ~ Philemon and Onesimus

Paul, a prisoner...

OPENING PRAYER
READ: Philemon 1-25

1) How do you characterize Onesimus before he was saved? _____
_____

2) Why did Paul not keep Onesimus with him? _____
_____

3) How was Paul willing to pay Onesimus' debt to Philemon? _____
_____
_____

Explore God's World

MEMORY VERSES:
Matthew 5:9-10 "Blessed are the peacemakers, for they shall be called sons of God. [10] Blessed are those who are persecuted for righteousness' sake, for theirs is the Kingdom of Heaven."

NAMES OF JESUS CHRIST IN THE BIBLE
41) **King of Israel** (Matthew 27:42),
42) **King of Kings** (1 Timothy 6:15; Revelation 19:16),
43) **Lamb of God** (John 1:29),
44) **Last Adam** (1 Corinthians 15:45),
45) **Life** (John 11:25),
46) **Light of the World** (John 8:12; John 9:5),
47) **Lord of Lords** (1 Timothy 6:15),
48) **Master** (Matthew 23:8)

For Your Information

FUN FACTS	THE TEN SMALLEST COUNTRIES IN THE WORLD BY AREA	JAMES THE SON OF ZEBEDEE
1. It took only 300 Israelite men under the leadership of Gideon to defeat 135,000 Midianites. 2. Cuba is the second in cane-sugar production in the world, while India is the first in cane-sugar production. 3. The Eiffel Tower was built by Alexandre Gustave Eiffel, a French civil engineer and architect.	1) Vatican City 2) Monaco 3) Nauru 4) Tuvalu 5) San Marino 6) Liechtenstein 7) Marshall Islands 8) Saint Kitts and Nevis 9) Maldives 10) Malta	…was one of Jesus' disciples, the brother of John the Apostle, and the partner of Peter. Both brothers were part of Jesus' inner circle. The mother of James and John overstepped her bounds in asking Jesus to grant her sons special positions in his Kingdom. James was the first of the apostles to be martyred (Acts 12).

GROUP DISCUSSION AND CLOSING PRAYER

"Education is an ornament in prosperity and a refuge in adversity."

Aristotle

Day 51 ~ Jesus Christ Is Superior over the Angels

God, who at...

OPENING PRAYER

READ: Hebrews 1:1-14 and 2:5-18

1) What is the function of the angels? _____

_____

2) Why were the angels not to be worshipped? _____

_____

3) What can you learn from 2:6-8? _____

_____

Explore God's World

MEMORY VERSES:

Matthew 5:9-10 "Blessed are the peacemakers, for they shall be called sons of God. ¹⁰ Blessed are those who are persecuted for righteousness' sake, for theirs is the Kingdom of Heaven."

NAMES OF JESUS CHRIST IN THE BIBLE

41) **King of Israel** (Matthew 27:42),
42) **King of Kings** (1 Timothy 6:15; Revelation 19:16),
43) **Lamb of God** (John 1:29),
44) **Last Adam** (1 Corinthians 15:45),
45) **Life** (John 11:25),
46) **Light of the World** (John 8:12; John 9:5),
47) **Lord of Lords** (1 Timothy 6:15),
48) **Master** (Matthew 23:8)

For Your Information

FUN FACTS	THE TEN SMALLEST COUNTRIES IN THE WORLD BY AREA	JOHN THE APOSTLE
1. Thailand is known as the Land of White Elephant. 2. The book of Obadiah is the shortest book in the Old Testament, while 3rd John is the shortest book in the whole Bible.	1) Vatican City 2) Monaco 3) Nauru 4) Tuvalu 5) San Marino 6) Liechtenstein 7) Marshall Islands 8) Saint Kitts and Nevis 9) Maldives 10) Malta	…brother of James, son of Zebedee, had the distinction of being the beloved friend of Jesus Christ. John is credited with writing the Gospel of John, 1st, 2nd, and 3rd John, and the book of Revelation. Dying of old age while he was in exile on the island of Patmos, he supposedly outlived all of the disciples.

GROUP DISCUSSION AND CLOSING PRAYER

"Start where you are. Use what you have. Do what you can."

Arthur Ashe

Day 52 ~ Christ's Superiority over Moses and Aaronic Priests

OPENING PRAYER
READ: Hebrews 3:1-15 and 4:1-13

Therefore, holy brethren,...

1) What was Moses' position in the building of God's house? _____
_____

2) How does the author of Hebrews describe "Today" and what you can learn? _____
_____

3) Describe the power of the Word of God. _____
_____

Explore God's World

MEMORY VERSES:

Matthew 5:9-10 "Blessed are the peacemakers, for they shall be called sons of God. [10] Blessed are those who are persecuted for righteousness' sake, for theirs is the Kingdom of Heaven."

NAMES OF JESUS CHRIST IN THE BIBLE
41) **King of Israel** (Matthew 27:42),
42) **King of Kings** (1 Timothy 6:15; Revelation 19:16),
43) **Lamb of God** (John 1:29),
44) **Last Adam** (1 Corinthians 15:45),
45) **Life** (John 11:25),
46) **Light of the World** (John 8:12; John 9:5),
47) **Lord of Lords** (1 Timothy 6:15),
48) **Master** (Matthew 23:8)

For Your Information

FUN FACTS	THE TEN SMALLEST COUNTRIES IN THE WORLD BY AREA	PHILIP
1. The Israelites celebrate 7 feast days of the Lord. 2. The name given to the border which separates Pakistan and Afghanistan is called the "Durand Line" (1,640 mi or 2640 km), which was named after Sir Mortimer Durand in 1983.	1) Vatican City 2) Monaco 3) Nauru 4) Tuvalu 5) San Marino 6) Liechtenstein 7) Marshall Islands 8) Saint Kitts and Nevis 9) Maldives 10) Malta	…was a Galilean, from the village of Bethsaida. Jesus issued a personal call to Philip: "Follow me." John 1:45-46 indicates he was well versed in Scripture (OT), yet he asked Jesus to show him the Father. Like the other apostles, he deserted Jesus during his trial and crucifixion. The last we hear of him is in the book of Acts on the day of Pentecost and at Jesus' ascension. The Apostle Philip is not Philip the Evangelist (one of the chosen seven deacons in the book of Acts)

GROUP DISCUSSION AND CLOSING PRAYER

"Success has many fathers, but failure is an orphan."

Unknown

Day 53 ~ Qualifications of a Priest

OPENING PRAYER
READ: Hebrews 5:1-14

For every high...

1) What two things were every Aaronic high priest expected to do? _____
_____

2) What can you learn from verse 9? _____
_____

3) What diet do some Christians need for their immaturity? _____
_____

Explore God's World

MEMORY VERSES:
Matthew 5:9-10 "Blessed are the peacemakers, for they shall be called sons of God. [10] Blessed are those who are persecuted for righteousness' sake, for theirs is the Kingdom of Heaven."

NAMES OF JESUS CHRIST IN THE BIBLE
41) **King of Israel** (Matthew 27:42),
42) **King of Kings** (1 Timothy 6:15; Revelation 19:16),
43) **Lamb of God** (John 1:29),
44) **Last Adam** (1 Corinthians 15:45),
45) **Life** (John 11:25),
46) **Light of the World** (John 8:12; John 9:5),
47) **Lord of Lords** (1 Timothy 6:15),
48) **Master** (Matthew 23:8)

For Your Information

FUN FACTS

1. It took only 300 Israelite men under the leadership of Gideon to defeat 135,000 Midianites.
2. Cuba is the second in cane-sugar production in the world, while India is the first in cane-sugar production.
3. The Eiffel Tower was built by Alexandre Gustave Eiffel, a French civil engineer and architect.

THE TEN SMALLEST COUNTRIES IN THE WORLD BY AREA

1) Vatican City
2) Monaco
3) Nauru
4) Tuvalu
5) San Marino
6) Liechtenstein
7) Marshall Islands
8) Saint Kitts and Nevis
9) Maldives
10) Malta

NATHANAEL

...one of the 12 disciples of Jesus Christ. His name means "gift of God." Most Bible scholars believe Nathanael and Bartholomew were the same person. The name Bartholomew is a family designation meaning "son of Tolmai." When told that the Messiah had been found, Nathanael questioned if "anything good" can come out of Nazareth, but soon acknowledged that Jesus was the Son of God and King of Israel. Very little is written about him in the Gospels.

GROUP DISCUSSION AND CLOSING PRAYER

*"We can easily forgive a child who is afraid of the dark;
the real tragedy of life is when men are afraid of the light."*

Plato

Day 54 ~ God's Promise & Christ's Superior Priestly Order

OPENING PRAYER
READ: Hebrews 6:1-18 and 7:1-10

Therefore, leaving the...

1) What are the elementary principles of Christ? _____
_____

2) What promise did God make with Abraham? _____
_____

3) Who is Melchizedek, and how does the Bible present him? _____
_____
_____

Explore God's World

MEMORY VERSES:
Matthew 5:9-10 "Blessed are the peacemakers, for they shall be called sons of God. [10] Blessed are those who are persecuted for righteousness' sake, for theirs is the Kingdom of Heaven."

NAMES OF JESUS CHRIST IN THE BIBLE
41) **King of Israel** (Matthew 27:42),
42) **King of Kings** (1 Timothy 6:15; Revelation 19:16),
43) **Lamb of God** (John 1:29),
44) **Last Adam** (1 Corinthians 15:45),
45) **Life** (John 11:25),
46) **Light of the World** (John 8:12; John 9:5),
47) **Lord of Lords** (1 Timothy 6:15),
48) **Master** (Matthew 23:8)

For Your Information

FUN FACTS	THE TEN SMALLEST COUNTRIES IN THE WORLD BY AREA	THOMAS
1. Thailand is known as the Land of White Elephant. 2. The book of Obadiah is the shortest book in the Old Testament, while 3rd John is the shortest book in the whole Bible.	1) Vatican City 2) Monaco 3) Nauru 4) Tuvalu 5) San Marino 6) Liechtenstein 7) Marshall Islands 8) Saint Kitts and Nevis 9) Maldives 10) Malta	...one of Jesus' 12 disciples, was not present when the risen Jesus first appeared to the disciples. When told by the others, "We have seen the Lord," Thomas replied that he would not believe them unless he could actually touch Jesus' wounds. Eight days later when he saw Jesus, he said, "My Lord and my God." Although the term is not used in the Bible, the nickname "Doubting Thomas" was given to this disciple because of his disbelief about the resurrection. People who are skeptical are sometimes referred to as "Doubting Thomas'."

GROUP DISCUSSION AND CLOSING PRAYER

"Believe you can and you're halfway there."
Theodore Roosevelt

Day 55 ~ The New Covenant and New Tabernacle

OPENING PRAYER
READ: Hebrews 8:1-13 and 9:1-15

Now this is the...

1) What was required from the new priestly order?_____
_____

2) What does the New Covenant represent?_____
_____

3) What was found in the Heavenly Sanctuary?_____
_____
_____

Explore God's World

MEMORY VERSES:

Matthew 5:9-10 "Blessed are the peacemakers, for they shall be called sons of God. [10] Blessed are those who are persecuted for righteousness' sake, for theirs is the Kingdom of Heaven."

NAMES OF JESUS CHRIST IN THE BIBLE
41) **King of Israel** (Matthew 27:42),
42) **King of Kings** (1 Timothy 6:15; Revelation 19:16),
43) **Lamb of God** (John 1:29),
44) **Last Adam** (1 Corinthians 15:45),
45) **Life** (John 11:25),
46) **Light of the World** (John 8:12; John 9:5),
47) **Lord of Lords** (1 Timothy 6:15),
48) **Master** (Matthew 23:8)

For Your Information

FUN FACTS	THE TEN SMALLEST COUNTRIES IN THE WORLD BY AREA	MATTHEW
1. The Israelites celebrate 7 feast days of the Lord. 2. The name given to the border which separates Pakistan and Afghanistan is called the "Durand Line" (1,640 mi or 2640 km), which was named after Sir Mortimer Durand in 1983.	1) Vatican City 2) Monaco 3) Nauru 4) Tuvalu 5) San Marino 6) Liechtenstein 7) Marshall Islands 8) Saint Kitts and Nevis 9) Maldives 10) Malta	…was a dishonest tax collector from Capernaum driven by greed, until Jesus Christ chose him as a disciple. He was named Levi before his call by Jesus. We don't know whether Jesus renamed him or whether he named himself Matthew, which is a shortening of Mattathias, meaning "the gift of God." He wrote the book of Matthew focusing on Jesus as King, the promised Messiah.

GROUP DISCUSSION AND CLOSING PRAYER

"Certain things catch your eye, but pursue only those that capture the heart."
Ancient Indian Proverb

Day 56 ~ *Week in Review*

TRUE OR FALSE — Circle T for true or F for false

T or F   Mark is short for the name Mattathias, which means "the gift of God."

T or F   James was one of Jesus' disciples.

T or F   The name given to the border which separates Iraq and Iran is called the "Durand Line".

T or F   "Success has many fathers, but failure is an orphan."

T or F   Singapore is known as the Land of White Elephant.

T or F   John had the distinction of being the beloved friend of Jesus Christ.

T or F   Cuba is the 2nd tea producer in the world, while India is 1st in coffee production.

T or F   Thomas was not present when the risen Jesus first appeared to the disciples.

T or F   The apostle Philip was also Jesus' younger brother.

T or F   The book of Obadiah is the shortest book in the Old Testament.

FILL IN THE BLANKS

a. People who are_____ are sometimes referred to as "_____Thomas."

b. The Israelites _____ 7 _____ days of the _____ .

c. The _____ given to the _____which_____Pakistan and_____ is called _____ Line.

d. James was the _____ of the _____ to be _____ (_____12).

e. Philip was a _____ from the _____of _____.

f. _____ of old_____ while John the _____was in exile on the _____ of Patmos.

g. Thailand is _____ as the _____ of the White _____.

h. Most _____ scholars_____ Nathanael and_____ were the _____person.

i. It took_____Israelite men under the_____ of_____to defeat_____ Midianites.

MEMORIZE AND WRITE

Matthew 5:9-10_____

_____

_____

_____

_____

MATCH THE FOLLOWING

_____ a. Nathanael   1. Alexandre Gustave Eiffel

_____ b. Obadiah   2. 135,000 Midianites

_____ c. Pakistan and Afghanistan   3. 7 feast days

_____ d. Thomas   4. Whole Bible

_____ e. Eiffel Tower   5. Gift of God

_____ f. Thailand   6. White Elephant

_____ g. Israelites   7. Tax collector

_____ h. 300 Israelites   8. Doubting Thomas

_____ i. 3rd John   9. Sir Mortimer Durand

_____ j. Matthew   10. Shortest book in the Bible

LIST THE TEN SMALLEST COUNTRIES IN THE WORLD BY AREA

1. _____   2. _____

3. _____   4. _____

5. _____   6. _____

7. _____   8. _____

9. _____   10. _____

LIST THE NAMES OF JESUS CHRIST IN THE BIBLE

1. _____   2. _____

3. _____   4. _____

5. _____   6. _____

7. _____   8. _____

CHRIST SUPERIOR ABOVE ALL

Through the book of Hebrews, the author took great lengths to show how far superior Christ is to anything created. He should have that same place in our lives. Examine yourself and write down things that you struggle to have Christ superior over.

_____

_____

_____

Angels Care for Jesus Coloring Activity

Note, you may make copies of this page to color if multiple family members in the same household want to color the illustration.

Day 57 ~ Faith Trained and Tested

OPENING PRAYER
READ: Hebrews 12:1-29

Therefore we also,...

1) Why is it so important for you to "look unto Jesus"? _____
_____

2) What did the Lord Jesus Christ endure that serves as the supreme example of faith? _____
_____

3) Why is pursuing holiness and peace with all people important for all believers? _____
_____
_____

Explore God's World

MEMORY VERSES:
Matthew 5:11-12 "Blessed are you when they revile and persecute you, and say all kinds of sake. [12] Rejoice and be exceedingly glad, for great is your reward in Heaven, for so they persecuted the prophets who were before you."

NAMES OF JESUS CHRIST IN THE BIBLE
49) Mediator (1st Timothy 2:5),
50) Messiah (John 1:41),
51) Mighty God (Isaiah 9:6),
52) Nazarene (Matthew 2:23),
53) Passover Lamb (1 Corinthians 5:7),
54) Physician (Matthew 9:12),
55) Potentate (1st Timothy 6:15),
56) Priest (Hebrews 4:15),
57) Prince of Peace (Isaiah 9:6)

For Your Information

FUN FACTS	THE FIVE COUNTRIES WITH THE MOST OLIVE OIL PRODUCTION	JAMES, SON OF ALPHAEUS
1. Abdul Salam was the first Pakistani to receive the Noble Peace Prize. 2. Margaret Thatcher was the first female Prime Minister of Britain. 3. The first rainbow appeared after Noah's flood was a sign of a covenant between God and earth	1) Spain 2) Italy 3) Greece 4) Turkey 5) Syria	...also known as James the Less, is not to be confused with James the son of Zebedee, brother of the Apostle John. James of Alphaeus is ninth in every listing of the 12 disciples. He was present with the 11 apostles in the upper room of Jerusalem after Christ ascended to heaven.

GROUP DISCUSSION AND CLOSING PRAYER

"Don't bother people for help without first trying to solve the problem yourself."
Colin Powell

Day 58 ~ Faith at Work

OPENING PRAYER
READ: Hebrews 13:1-19

Let brotherly love...

1) What did Jesus mean when He said "I will never leave you nor forsake you"? _____
_____

2) What is God's view of Christian marriage? _____
_____

3) What is so unique about Jesus Christ? _____
_____
_____
_____

Explore God's World

MEMORY VERSES:

Matthew 5:11-12 "Blessed are you when they revile and persecute you, and say all kinds of sake. [12] Rejoice and be exceedingly glad, for great is your reward in Heaven, for so they persecuted the prophets who were before you."

NAMES OF JESUS CHRIST IN THE BIBLE
49) Mediator (1st Timothy 2:5),
50) Messiah (John 1:41),
51) Mighty God (Isaiah 9:6),
52) Nazarene (Matthew 2:23),
53) Passover Lamb (1 Corinthians 5:7),
54) Physician (Matthew 9:12),
55) Potentate (1st Timothy 6:15),
56) Priest (Hebrews 4:15),
57) Prince of Peace (Isaiah 9:6)

For Your Information

FUN FACTS	THE FIVE COUNTRIES WITH THE MOST OLIVE OIL PRODUCTION	JUDE
1. London University was the first British university to admit women for degree courses. 2. Ralph Johnson Bunche was the first African American to be awarded the Noble Peace Prize. 3. Jacob's name was changed to Israel after he wrestled with an angel, and he called the place where they wrestled Peniel.	1) Spain 2) Italy 3) Greece 4) Turkey 5) Syria	…was among the disciples/followers of Jesus and the brother of James, thus, half brother to Jesus Christ, whom he accepted as the Messiah after Jesus' resurrection. He is called Thaddeus or Thaddaeus, a surname for the name Lebbaeus (Matthew 10:3), which means "heart" or "courageous." Very little is known about him other than he authored, the single epistle by his name. He calls himself "Jude, a servant of Jesus Christ and a brother of James." The final two verses of Jude (24-25) contain a doxology, or "expression of praise to God," considered the finest in the New Testament.

GROUP DISCUSSION AND CLOSING PRAYER

"It's how you deal with failure that determines how you achieve success."

Charlotte Whitton

Day 59 ~ Trials & Temptation

OPENING PRAYER
READ: James 1:1-27

James, a servant...

1) Which James was the writer of this epistle? _____
_____

2) What does "testing of your faith produces" mean? _____
_____

3) Explain "God is tempting me." _____
_____
_____

Explore God's World

MEMORY VERSES:

Matthew 5:11-12 "Blessed are you when they revile and persecute you, and say all kinds of sake. ¹² Rejoice and be exceedingly glad, for great is your reward in Heaven, for so they persecuted the prophets who were before you."

NAMES OF JESUS CHRIST IN THE BIBLE
49) Mediator (1st Timothy 2:5),
50) Messiah (John 1:41),
51) Mighty God (Isaiah 9:6),
52) Nazarene (Matthew 2:23),
53) Passover Lamb (1 Corinthians 5:7),
54) Physician (Matthew 9:12),
55) Potentate (1st Timothy 6:15),
56) Priest (Hebrews 4:15),
57) Prince of Peace (Isaiah 9:6)

For Your Information

FUN FACTS	THE FIVE COUNTRIES WITH THE MOST OLIVE OIL PRODUCTION	MARY MAGDALENE
1. Formosa is the old name of Taiwan. 2. Scotland is known as the Land of Cakes. 3. While being stoned, Stephen, as he looked up, saw Jesus standing at the right hand of the Father	1) Spain 2) Italy 3) Greece 4) Turkey 5) Syria	...was delivered from seven demons by Jesus Christ. After that, she, along with several other women, became followers of Jesus. She proved to be more loyal to Jesus than his own Apostles. Instead of hiding, she stood near the cross as He died. She went to the tomb to anoint his body with spices. Mary's great faith earned her special affection from Jesus.

GROUP DISCUSSION AND CLOSING PRAYER

"Education is the most powerful weapon which you can use to change the world."
Nelson Mandela

Day 60 ~ Partiality Versus Obedience

My brothers and...

OPENING PRAYER
READ: James 2:1-26

1) Why is favoritism prohibited in the church? What should Christians do?_____
_____

2) What is the "royal law" and to whom does it apply?_____
_____

3) Does faith require deeds? How must a fellow Christian act?_____
_____
_____

Explore God's World

MEMORY VERSES:

Matthew 5:11-12

"Blessed are you when they revile and persecute you, and say all kinds of sake. [12] Rejoice and be exceedingly glad, for great is your reward in Heaven, for so they persecuted the prophets who were before you."

NAMES OF JESUS CHRIST IN THE BIBLE

49) Mediator (1st Timothy 2:5),
50) Messiah (John 1:41),
51) Mighty God (Isaiah 9:6),
52) Nazarene (Matthew 2:23),
53) Passover Lamb (1 Corinthians 5:7),
54) Physician (Matthew 9:12),
55) Potentate (1st Timothy 6:15),
56) Priest (Hebrews 4:15),
57) Prince of Peace (Isaiah 9:6)

For Your Information

FUN FACTS	THE FIVE COUNTRIES WITH THE MOST OLIVE OIL PRODUCTION	PONTIUS PILATE
1. Abdul Salam was the first Pakistani to receive the Noble Peace Prize. 2. Margaret Thatcher was the first female Prime Minister of Britain. 3. The first rainbow appeared after Noah's flood was a sign of a covenant between God and earth	1) Spain 2) Italy 3) Greece 4) Turkey 5) Syria	...was a key figure in the trial of Jesus. In the Gospels, he is portrayed as finding no fault with Jesus and symbolically washes his hands of the matter. Yet seeing the Sanhedrin rile the people against Jesus, Pilate feared the unrest among the Jews would result in a revolt against the Roman rule, thus costing him his position, so he gave in to the crowd and allowed Jesus to be crucified.

GROUP DISCUSSION AND CLOSING PRAYER

"Heroes may not be braver than anyone else. They're just braver five minutes longer."

Ronald Reagan

Day 61 ~ Speech & Obedience

OPENING PRAYER
READ: James 3:1-18

My brethren, let...

1) Why will teachers of the Scriptures be judged more strictly?_____
_____

2) What are two kinds of wisdom?_____
_____

3) What can the untamed tongue do? List a few._____
_____
_____

Explore God's World

MEMORY VERSES:
Matthew 5:11-12 "Blessed are you when they revile and persecute you, and say all kinds of sake. ¹² Rejoice and be exceedingly glad, for great is your reward in Heaven, for so they persecuted the prophets who were before you."

NAMES OF JESUS CHRIST IN THE BIBLE
49) Mediator (1st Timothy 2:5),
50) Messiah (John 1:41),
51) Mighty God (Isaiah 9:6),
52) Nazarene (Matthew 2:23),
53) Passover Lamb (1 Corinthians 5:7),
54) Physician (Matthew 9:12),
55) Potentate (1st Timothy 6:15),
56) Priest (Hebrews 4:15),
57) Prince of Peace (Isaiah 9:6)

For Your Information

FUN FACTS	THE FIVE COUNTRIES WITH THE MOST OLIVE OIL PRODUCTION	JOSEPH OF ARIMATHEA
1. London University was the first British university to admit women for degree courses. 2. Ralph Johnson Bunche was the first African American to be awarded the Noble Peace Prize. 3. Jacob's name was changed to Israel after he wrestled with an angel, and he called the place where they wrestled Peniel.	1) Spain 2) Italy 3) Greece 4) Turkey 5) Syria	…was a prominent member of the Sanhedrin, the Jewish religious council which sought the death of Jesus. However, he risked his reputation and life by standing up for Jesus because of his faith as a secret believer in Jesus far outweighed his fear of his colleagues. Matthew calls him a "rich" man, who donated his new tomb for Jesus to be buried in, while Luke calls Joseph of Arimathea a "good and upright man."

GROUP DISCUSSION AND CLOSING PRAYER

"History is written by the winners."

Alex Haley

Day 62 ~ Witnessing to Divine Providence

OPENING PRAYER
READ: James 4:5-16 and 5:1-12

And when He had...

1) To whom is more grace given? What does it bring forth? _____
_____

2) How should a Christian see tomorrow? Of which things should he boast? _____
_____

3) How shall rich oppressors be judged? _____
_____
_____

Explore God's World

MEMORY VERSES:
Matthew 5:11-12 "Blessed are you when they revile and persecute you, and say all kinds of sake. [12] Rejoice and be exceedingly glad, for great is your reward in Heaven, for so they persecuted the prophets who were before you."

NAMES OF JESUS CHRIST IN THE BIBLE
49) Mediator (1st Timothy 2:5),
50) Messiah (John 1:41),
51) Mighty God (Isaiah 9:6),
52) Nazarene (Matthew 2:23),
53) Passover Lamb (1 Corinthians 5:7),
54) Physician (Matthew 9:12),
55) Potentate (1st Timothy 6:15),
56) Priest (Hebrews 4:15),
57) Prince of Peace (Isaiah 9:6)

For Your Information

FUN FACTS	THE FIVE COUNTRIES WITH THE MOST OLIVE OIL PRODUCTION	NICODEMUS
1. Formosa is the old name of Taiwan. 2. Scotland is known as the Land of Cakes. 3. While being stoned, Stephen, as he looked up, saw Jesus standing at the right hand of the Father	1) Spain 2) Italy 3) Greece 4) Turkey 5) Syria	...was a Pharisee who was not satisfied with legalism. As a member of the Sanhedrin, he secretly visited Jesus to inquire about the new birth that Jesus was teaching. As the Sanhedrin was plotting the death of Jesus, Nicodemus questioned the Council's judging Jesus before hearing His defense. At great risk to his safety and reputation, Nicodemus provided rich spices for Jesus' embalmment, boldly helped Joseph of Arimathea take Jesus' body down from the cross, and placed it in the tomb donated by his fellow councilman.

GROUP DISCUSSION AND CLOSING PRAYER

"You can accomplish anything in life provided you don't mind who gets the credit."
Harry S. Truman

Day 63 ~ Week in Review

MEMORIZE AND WRITE

Matthew 5:11-12 _____

_____

_____

TRUE OR FALSE — Circle T for true or F for false

T or F   Ralph Johnson Bunche was the first Cuban to be awarded the Noble Peace Prize.

T or F   The first rainbow appeared after Noah's flood as a sign of covenant.

T or F   Ireland is known as the Land of Cakes.

T or F   Margaret Thatcher was the first female Prime Minister of Britain.

T or F   Joseph of Arimathea was a prominent member of the Sanhedrin.

T or F   Abdul Salam was the 1st Bangladeshi to receive the Noble Peace Prize.

T or F   London University was the first British university to admit women for degree courses.

T or F   Nicodemus was a Pharisee and was very happy with their legalism.

T or F   Formosa is the old name of Thailand.

MATCH THE FOLLOWING

_____ a. Formosa   1. Prime Minister

_____ b. Jacob   2. Admit women

_____ c. Ralph Johnson Bunche   3. Noah's flood

_____ d. Mary Magdalene   4. Land of Cakes

_____ e. 1st rainbow   5. Sanhedrin

_____ f. Margaret Thatcher   6. Peniel

_____ g. Joseph of Arimathea   7. Seven demons

_____ h. London University   8. Noble Peace Prize

_____ i. Scotland   9. Taiwan

LIST THE FIVE COUNTRIES WITH THE MOST OLIVE OIL PRODUCTION

1._____   2._____

3._____   4._____

5._____

FILL IN THE BLANKS

a. _____ Magdalene was _____ from seven _____ by Jesus Christ.

b. London _____ was the first British _____ to admit_____ for _____ courses.

c. James, son of _____, was also known as_____ the _____.

d. Scotland is _____ as the_____ of _____ .

e. Pontius _____ was a key _____ in the trial of_____ .

f. Abdul _____ was the first _____ to receive the_____ Prize.

g. Nicodemus was a _____ and was not _____ with their _____.

h. Margaret _____ was the _____ female Prime _____ of _____.

i. Ralph _____ Bunche was the _____ African _____ to be awarded the _____ Peace _____.

j. The _____ two _____ of Jude (24-25) contain a _____ , or "expression of _____ to _____ ."

LIST AND MEMORIZE NAMES OF JESUS CHRIST IN THE BIBLE

1. _____   2. _____

3. _____   4. _____

5. _____   6. _____

7. _____   8. _____

9. _____

GODLY LIVING

Our faith in Jesus Christ for salvation should make a practical difference. Regardless of what kind of situation we are in, through our thoughts, words and deeds our faith should be easily seen. Think and write down some ways your faith can be seen practically.

_____

_____

_____

_____

_____

_____

Following Jesus Coloring Activity

Note, you may make copies of this page to color if multiple family members in the same household want to color the illustration.

Day 64 ~ Comfort and Reassurance in Suffering

OPENING PRAYER
READ: 1st Peter 1:1-25

Peter, an apostle...

1) What does it take for a Christian to inherit Heaven?_____
_____

2) How does God our Father command us to live in this world?_____
_____

3) What attitude should Christians have toward other believers?_____
_____
_____

Explore God's World

MEMORY VERSES:

Proverbs 12:1 "Whoever loves instruction loves knowledge, but he who hates correction is stupid."

John 14:27 "Peace I leave with you, My peace I give to you; not as the world gives do I give to you. Let not your heart be troubled, neither let it be afraid."

NAMES OF JESUS CHRIST IN THE BIBLE

58) **Prophet** (Acts 3:22),
59) **Propitiation** (I John 2:2),
60) **Purifier** (Malachi 3:3),
61) **Rabbi** (John 1:49),
62) **Ransom** (1 Timothy 2:6),
63) **Redeemer** (Isaiah 41:14),
64) **Refiner** (Malachi 3:2),
65) **Refuge** (Isaiah 25:4),
66) **Resurrection** (John 11:25),
67) **Righteousness** (Jeremiah 23:6)

For Your Information

FUN FACTS	SEVEN COUNTRIES WITH THE HIGHEST WINE PRODUCTION	JOSEPH CAIAPHAS
1. Isaac M. Singer invented the sewing machine. 2. An earlier name for the tomato was love apple. 3. Jesus' last miracle before the crucifixion was healing Malchus' severed ear in Gethsemane.	1) Italy 2) France 3) Spain 4) United States 5) Argentina 6) Chile 7) Australia	...was head of the Sanhedrin in Jerusalem, and played a key role in the trial and execution of Jesus Christ. He accused Jesus of blasphemy, a crime punishable by death under Jewish law. But, as the council did not have the authority to execute people, he turned to the Roman governor, Pontius Pilate, who could carry out a death sentence. His argument to Pilate was that Jesus was a threat to Roman stability and, thus, had to die to prevent a rebellion.

GROUP DISCUSSION AND CLOSING PRAYER

"Great minds discuss ideas, average minds discuss events, small minds discuss people."

Eleanor Roosevelt

Day 65 ~ Practical Holiness

OPENING PRAYER

READ: 1st Peter 2:4-17 and 3:1-12

Coming to Him...

1) Why is Jesus called the Chief Cornerstone? _____

_____

2) How are wives commanded to live a Godly life? _____

_____

3) How are husbands commanded to treat their wives? _____

_____

_____

Explore God's World

MEMORY VERSES:

Proverbs 12:1 "Whoever loves instruction loves knowledge, but he who hates correction is stupid."

John 14:27 "Peace I leave with you, My peace I give to you; not as the world gives do I give to you. Let not your heart be troubled, neither let it be afraid."

NAMES OF JESUS CHRIST IN THE BIBLE
58) **Prophet** (Acts 3:22),
59) **Propitiation** (I John 2:2),
60) **Purifier** (Malachi 3:3),
61) **Rabbi** (John 1:49),
62) **Ransom** (1 Timothy 2:6),
63) **Redeemer** (Isaiah 41:14),
64) **Refiner** (Malachi 3:2),
65) **Refuge** (Isaiah 25:4),
66) **Resurrection** (John 11:25),
67) **Righteousness** (Jeremiah 23:6)

For Your Information

FUN FACTS	SEVEN COUNTRIES WITH THE HIGHEST WINE PRODUCTION	HEROD ANTIPAS
1. The literal meaning of renaissance is "rebirth". 2. Fallen angels are those who rebelled against God along with Lucifer, an archangel who became known as the devil. (Isaiah 14:12-14, Rev. 12:9)	1) Italy 2) France 3) Spain 4) United States 5) Argentina 6) Chile 7) Australia	...was one of the co-conspirators who carried out the condemnation and execution of Jesus Christ. More than 30 years earlier, his father, Herod the Great, had tried to murder the young Jesus by slaughtering all the boys under two years old in Bethlehem, but failed because Joseph and Mary had already fled to Egypt with the baby Jesus.

GROUP DISCUSSION AND CLOSING PRAYER

"One who is patient glows with an inner radiance."

Allan Lokos

Day 66 ~ The Spiritual Significance of Suffering

Therefore, since Christ...

OPENING PRAYER
READ: 1st Peter 4:1-16

1) Explain "spent enough of our past lifetime in doing the will of the Gentiles." _____
_____

2) Explain "love will cover a multitude of sins." _____
_____

3) What should Christians do in the midst of suffering? _____
_____

Explore God's World

MEMORY VERSES:

Proverbs 12:1 "Whoever loves instruction loves knowledge, but he who hates correction is stupid."

John 14:27 "Peace I leave with you, My peace I give to you; not as the world gives do I give to you. Let not your heart be troubled, neither let it be afraid."

NAMES OF JESUS CHRIST IN THE BIBLE
58) **Prophet** (Acts 3:22),
59) **Propitiation** (I John 2:2),
60) **Purifier** (Malachi 3:3),
61) **Rabbi** (John 1:49),
62) **Ransom** (1 Timothy 2:6),
63) **Redeemer** (Isaiah 41:14),
64) **Refiner** (Malachi 3:2),
65) **Refuge** (Isaiah 25:4),
66) **Resurrection** (John 11:25),
67) **Righteousness** (Jeremiah 23:6)

For Your Information

FUN FACTS	SEVEN COUNTRIES WITH THE HIGHEST WINE PRODUCTION	PAUL
1. "Goodbye" came from the words "God be with you." 2. Heresy is a teaching that deviates from the truth of Biblical revelation. It is a false teaching. The word occurs 9 times in the New Testament and is translated as "sect."	1) Italy 2) France 3) Spain 4) United States 5) Argentina 6) Chile 7) Australia	…was also known as Saul of Tarsus, a zealous Pharisee, bent on killing believers in Jesus Christ. On one of his journeys to arrest Christians, he encountered the resurrected Jesus Christ on the Damascus road. The experience blinded him until Ananias was sent by God to heal Saul's eyes. He was renamed Paul afterward. Paul is taught, in the desert of Saudi Arabia, by Jesus Himself. Paul made three missionary journeys throughout the Roman Empire. Thirteen books in the New Testament are identified with Paul, who had a brilliant mind because of his commanding knowledge of philosophy and religion. He was so well-versed that he could debate with the most educated scholars of his day.

GROUP DISCUSSION AND CLOSING PRAYER

"Good friends are hard to find, harder to leave, and impossible to forget."

Anonymous

Day 67 ~ False Prophets and Teachers

OPENING PRAYER
READ: 2nd Peter 2:1-22

But there were...

1) Who are the ones that deny our Lord Jesus Christ? _____
_____

2) What happened to the cities of Sodom and Gomorrah? _____
_____

3) How does Peter describe the false teachers? _____
_____

Explore God's World

MEMORY VERSES:

Proverbs 12:1 "Whoever loves instruction loves knowledge, but he who hates correction is stupid."

John 14:27 "Peace I leave with you, My peace I give to you; not as the world gives do I give to you. Let not your heart be troubled, neither let it be afraid."

NAMES OF JESUS CHRIST IN THE BIBLE
58) **Prophet** (Acts 3:22),
59) **Propitiation** (I John 2:2),
60) **Purifier** (Malachi 3:3),
61) **Rabbi** (John 1:49),
62) **Ransom** (1 Timothy 2:6),
63) **Redeemer** (Isaiah 41:14),
64) **Refiner** (Malachi 3:2),
65) **Refuge** (Isaiah 25:4),
66) **Resurrection** (John 11:25),
67) **Righteousness** (Jeremiah 23:6)

For Your Information

FUN FACTS
1. Isaac M. Singer invented the sewing machine.
2. An earlier name for the tomato was love apple.
3. Jesus' last miracle before the crucifixion was healing Malchus' severed ear in Gethsemane.

SEVEN COUNTRIES WITH THE HIGHEST WINE PRODUCTION
1) Italy
2) France 3) Spain
4) United States
5) Argentina
6) Chile 7) Australia

LUKE
...authored not only the gospel bearing his name, but also Acts, which scholars attribute to him. Some credit Luke's training as a medical doctor for his attention to accuracy. A Gentile, probably a Greek, he may have been converted to Christianity by Paul, with whom he endured the hardships of travel and persecution.

GROUP DISCUSSION AND CLOSING PRAYER

"There is only one way to avoid criticism: do nothing, say nothing, and be nothing."
Aristotle

Day 68 ~ The Fact of Christ's Return

Beloved, I now...

OPENING PRAYER
READ: 2nd Peter 3:1-18

1) What was the reason that Peter wrote 2nd Peter to the believers? _____
_____

2) How will the Day of the Lord come? _____
_____

3) What can you learn from verse 12? _____
_____
_____

Explore God's World

MEMORY VERSES:

Proverbs 12:1 "Whoever loves instruction loves knowledge, but he who hates correction is stupid."

John 14:27 "Peace I leave with you, My peace I give to you; not as the world gives do I give to you. Let not your heart be troubled, neither let it be afraid."

NAMES OF JESUS CHRIST IN THE BIBLE
58) **Prophet** (Acts 3:22),
59) **Propitiation** (I John 2:2),
60) **Purifier** (Malachi 3:3),
61) **Rabbi** (John 1:49),
62) **Ransom** (1 Timothy 2:6),
63) **Redeemer** (Isaiah 41:14),
64) **Refiner** (Malachi 3:2),
65) **Refuge** (Isaiah 25:4),
66) **Resurrection** (John 11:25),
67) **Righteousness** (Jeremiah 23:6)

For Your Information

FUN FACTS	SEVEN COUNTRIES WITH THE HIGHEST WINE PRODUCTION	JOHN MARK
1. The literal meaning of renaissance is "rebirth". 2. Fallen angels are those who rebelled against God along with Lucifer, an archangel who became known as the devil. (Isaiah 14:12-14, Rev. 12:9)	1) Italy 2) France 3) Spain 4) United States 5) Argentina 6) Chile 7) Australia	...the author of the Gospel of Mark, served as a companion to the Apostle Paul in his missionary work and later assisted Peter in Rome. According to Coptic tradition, John Mark was the founder of the Coptic Church in Egypt. Coptics believe Mark was tied to a horse and dragged to his death by a mob of Alexandrian pagans on Easter in 68 A.D.

GROUP DISCUSSION AND CLOSING PRAYER

"I never learn anything talking. I only learn things when I ask questions."

Lou Holtz

Day 69 ~ Walking in the Light & Knowing Your Spiritual Status

OPENING PRAYER
READ: 1st John 1:1-8 and 2:1-17

That which was...

1) How can you deceive your own self?_____

_____

2) What is the function of an advocate in our lives?_____

_____

3) Why is it important "not to love the world"?_____

_____

Explore God's World

MEMORY VERSES:

Proverbs 12:1 "Whoever loves instruction loves knowledge, but he who hates correction is stupid."

John 14:27 "Peace I leave with you, My peace I give to you; not as the world gives do I give to you. Let not your heart be troubled, neither let it be afraid."

NAMES OF JESUS CHRIST IN THE BIBLE

58) **Prophet** (Acts 3:22),
59) **Propitiation** (I John 2:2),
60) **Purifier** (Malachi 3:3),
61) **Rabbi** (John 1:49),
62) **Ransom** (1 Timothy 2:6),
63) **Redeemer** (Isaiah 41:14),
64) **Refiner** (Malachi 3:2),
65) **Refuge** (Isaiah 25:4),
66) **Resurrection** (John 11:25),
67) **Righteousness** (Jeremiah 23:6)

For Your Information

FUN FACTS	SEVEN COUNTRIES WITH THE HIGHEST WINE PRODUCTION	BARNABAS
1. "Goodbye" came from the words "God be with you." 2. Heresy is a teaching that deviates from the truth of Biblical revelation. It is a false teaching. The word occurs 9 times in the New Testament and is translated as "sect."	1) Italy 2) France 3) Spain 4) United States 5) Argentina 6) Chile 7) Australia	…means "son of encouragement," a title that he no doubt earned by building up and encouraging individuals as well as the members of struggling young churches. As "a good man and full of the Holy Ghost and of faith" (Acts 11:24), he gave the money he received from the sale of a field to the apostles to aid the poorer members in the Jerusalem church. Because of Barnabas' defense of the converted Paul, the members in Jerusalem were convinced to accept the once "persecutor of Christians" into their fellowship, thus, helping to make possible Paul's missionary journeys and epistles. Barnabas defended and encouraged John Mark, author of the Gospel of Mark. His faith sustained him despite persecution.

GROUP DISCUSSION AND CLOSING PRAYER

"Rules cannot take the place of character."

Alan Greenspan

Helping Parents Develop Their Children's Love for God and for People

Day 70 ~ Week in Review

MATCH THE FOLLOWING

_____ a. Goodbye		1. A Gentile and Greek
_____ b. Renaissance		2. Love Apple
_____ c. Joseph Caiaphas		3. False teaching
_____ d. Fallen angels		4. Sewing Machine
_____ e. Tomato		5. Malchus' ear
_____ f. Luke		6. Revival
_____ g. Jesus' last miracle		7. Sanhedrin
_____ h. Isaac M. Singer		8. Devil
_____ i. Heresy		9. God be with you

TRUE OR FALSE — Circle T for true or F for false

T or F   James is credited as the author of 11 of books in the New Testament.

T or F   "Goodbye" came from the words "God be with you."

T or F   John the Baptist is the founder of the Coptic Church in Egypt

T or F   Jesus' last miracle before the crucifixion was the raising of Lazarus in Gethsemane.

T or F   John Mark means "son of encouragement."

T or F   The earlier name for orange was Love Apple.

T or F   The literal meaning of renaissance is "rebirth."

T or F   Isaac M Singer invented the washing machine.

T or F   According to Coptic tradition, Paul was the founder of the Coptic Church in Egypt.

MEMORIZE AND WRITE THE NAMES OF JESUS CHRIST IN THE BIBLE

1. _____   2. _____

3. _____   4. _____

5. _____   6. _____

7. _____   8. _____

9. _____   10. _____

LIST SEVEN COUNTRIES WITH THE HIGHEST WINE PRODUCTION

1. _____   2. _____

3. _____   4. _____

5. _____   6. _____

7. _____

FILL IN THE BLANKS

a. Barnabas _____ "son of _____."

b. Jesus' _____ miracle before the _____ was _____ of _____ ear in _____.

c. The _____ meaning _____ renaissance is " _____."

d. Some _____ Luke's training as a medical _____ for his attention to _____.

e. Heresy is a _____ that _____ from the truth of _____ revelation. It is a false _____.

f. Isaac M _____ invented the _____ machine.

g. According to _____ tradition, John Mark was the _____ of the Coptic _____ in Egypt.

h. The _____ name for _____ was Love _____.

i. Paul _____ three _____ journeys _____ the Roman _____.

MEMORIZE AND WRITE

Proverbs 12:1 _____

_____

_____

John 14:27 _____

_____

_____

THE TRUTH ON SUFFERING

As believers our hope is one day we will be removed from all suffering that sin has caused in our lives. Meanwhile as we live in this world of sin, how can God use our suffering in our lives and those around us?

_____

_____

_____

Bible Word Search

```
R  E  K  L  A  W  C  A  L  B  C  S  E  R  X
N  E  S  P  K  E  N  G  R  X  O  S  A  Y  M
S  D  A  L  S  Y  G  O  H  A  R  E  B  G  J
R  D  U  S  A  I  H  K  C  F  N  N  V  R  Y
C  T  N  A  S  F  S  R  E  V  E  I  L  E  B
O  S  B  A  D  U  H  Z  S  T  R  L  S  E  W
M  X  G  E  B  E  R  U  Q  I  S  O  K  F  I
F  W  N  G  A  S  F  A  S  R  T  H  F  M  W
O  Y  I  V  O  F  U  R  N  H  O  L  O  V  E
R  E  E  L  E  M  E  H  G  C  N  J  G  A  U
T  N  U  R  L  H  O  I  M  S  E  V  I  W  M
D  I  I  V  C  P  L  R  G  T  K  S  M  D  O
U  N  F  A  N  U  S  H  R  H  W  I  J  R  D
G  D  E  U  S  O  A  U  D  A  Y  N  F  L  O
V  T  P  R  O  P  H  E  T  S  H  S  F  K  S
```

BELIEVERS	COMFORT	CORNERSTONE
DENY	FALSE	GOMORRAH
HEAVEN	HOLINESS	HUSBANDS
LIGHT	LOVE	PROPHETS
REASSURANCE	SINS	SODOM
SUFFERING	TEACHERS	WALK
WILL	WIVES	

Day 71 ~ God Is Love

OPENING PRAYER
READ: 1st John 3:1-24

Behold what manner...

1) What is sin, and where does it lead you?_____
_____

2) Who are the children of God? Who are the children of the devil?_____
_____

3) How can you abide in Christ and He in you?_____
_____

Explore God's World

MEMORY VERSES:

Psalms 55:22 "Cast your burden on the Lord, and He shall sustain you; He shall never permit the righteous to be moved."

Zechariah 4:6 So he answered and said to me: "This is the word of the Lord to Zerubbabel: 'Not by might nor by power, but by My Spirit,' says the Lord of hosts."

NAMES OF JESUS CHRIST IN THE BIBLE
68) **Rock** (Deuteronomy 32:4),
69) **Root of David** (Revelation 22:16),
70) **Rose of Sharon** (Song of Solomon 2:1),
71) **Sacrifice** (Ephesians 5:2),
72) **Savior** (2 Samuel 22:47; Luke 1:47),
73) **Last Adam** (1 Corinthians 15:45),
74) **Seed of Abraham** (Galatians 3:16),
75) **Seed of David** (2 Timothy 2:8)

For Your Information

FUN FACTS	THE TOP SEVEN POTATO PRODUCING COUNTRIES	PHILIP
1. Abraham Lincoln abolished the slavery in America. 2. Napoleon suffered from ailurophobia which means fear of cats. 3. The purpose of the Bible is to reveal the character of God, His will for mankind. His plan of Salvation for mankind through the Old Testament prophecies about the Messiah and the New Testament arrival of, the ministry and sacrifice of Jesus Christ who rose from the dead and ascended into Heaven until His second coming.	1) China 2) India 3) Russia 4) Ukraine 5) USA 6) Germany 7) Bangladesh	...was one of the seven deacons chosen to minister to Gentile widows, and he was also the first Christian to preach outside of Jerusalem (Acts 8), that is, in Samaria, capital of the hated Samaritans. By the guidance of the Holy Ghost, he was sent into the desert where he met and taught an Ethiopian official about God.

GROUP DISCUSSION AND CLOSING PRAYER

"If you judge people, you have no time to love them."

Mother Teresa

Day 72 ~ *Examining the Spirit*

Beloved, do not...

1) When will the spirit of the antichrist be present in the world? _____

_____

2) How can you be assured that God loves you? _____

_____

3) What is the sign of perfect love? _____

_____

Explore God's World

MEMORY VERSES:

Psalms 55:22 "Cast your burden on the Lord, and He shall sustain you; He shall never permit the righteous to be moved."

Zechariah 4:6 So he answered and said to me: "This is the word of the Lord to Zerubbabel: 'Not by might nor by power, but by My Spirit,' says the Lord of hosts."

NAMES OF JESUS CHRIST IN THE BIBLE

68) **Rock** (Deuteronomy 32:4),
69) **Root of David** (Revelation 22:16),
70) **Rose of Sharon** (Song of Solomon 2:1),
71) **Sacrifice** (Ephesians 5:2),
72) **Savior** (2 Samuel 22:47; Luke 1:47),
73) **Last Adam** (1 Corinthians 15:45),
74) **Seed of Abraham** (Galatians 3:16),
75) **Seed of David** (2 Timothy 2:8)

For Your Information

FUN FACTS	THE TOP SEVEN POTATO PRODUCING COUNTRIES	SIMON THE SORCERER
1. Rome was founded in the year 753 B.C. 2. Finland won independence in 1917 from Russia. 3. Designed by God, marriage is a "covenant union," not a "contract," between a man and a woman.	1) China 2) India 3) Russia 4) Ukraine 5) USA 6) Germany 7) Bangladesh	...was baptized by Philip the Evangelist. After his conversion, Simon tried to buy spiritual power from the apostles after he saw them laying hands on people to receive the Holy Spirit. (Acts 8) The sin of simony, or paying for position and influence in the church, is named for Simon the Sorcerer.

GROUP DISCUSSION AND CLOSING PRAYER

"The two most important days in your life are: the day you are born and the day you find out why."

Stephen King

Day 73 ~ Through Obedience Comes Blessings

OPENING PRAYER
READ: 1st John 5:1-25

Whoever believes...

1) Who are the three that bear witness in heaven and on earth?_____

_____

2) Who is the greater witness? How has his witness been proven greater?_____

_____

3) What is so unique about the One about whom John writes?_____

_____

_____

Explore God's World

MEMORY VERSES:

Psalms 55:22 "Cast your burden on the Lord, and He shall sustain you; He shall never permit the righteous to be moved."

Zechariah 4:6 So he answered and said to me: "This is the word of the Lord to Zerubbabel: 'Not by might nor by power, but by My Spirit,' says the Lord of hosts."

NAMES OF JESUS CHRIST IN THE BIBLE
68) **Rock** (Deuteronomy 32:4),
69) **Root of David** (Revelation 22:16),
70) **Rose of Sharon** (Song of Solomon 2:1),
71) **Sacrifice** (Ephesians 5:2),
72) **Savior** (2 Samuel 22:47; Luke 1:47),
73) **Last Adam** (1 Corinthians 15:45),
74) **Seed of Abraham** (Galatians 3:16),
75) **Seed of David** (2 Timothy 2:8)

For Your Information

FUN FACTS	THE TOP SEVEN POTATO PRODUCING COUNTRIES	TIMOTHY
1. A standard piano has 88 keys. 2. Montreal, Canada is the second largest French speaking city in the world. 3. There are 30 different types of precious stones mentioned in the Bible.	1) China 2) India 3) Russia 4) Ukraine 5) USA 6) Germany 7) Bangladesh	...is described as "honoring God" and being Paul's "true son in the faith." His Greek (Gentile) father is not mentioned by name, while Eunice, his Jewish mother, and his grandmother, Lois, taught him the Scriptures from the time he was a young boy. He accompanied Paul on his missionary journeys, and when Paul was in prison, Timothy represented Paul at Corinth and Philippi. For a time, Timothy was also imprisoned for the faith.

GROUP DISCUSSION AND CLOSING PRAYER

"Tolerance is nothing more than patience with boundaries."

Shannon L. Alder

Day 74 ~ Walking in the Light

OPENING PRAYER
READ: 2nd John 1-13

The Elder, To...

1) How is the grace from the Father and the Son given to us? _____
_____

2) Which commandment is given to all of us? _____
_____

3) Who is the antichrist and how will he deceive God's people? _____
_____

Explore God's World

MEMORY VERSES:

Psalms 55:22 "Cast your burden on the Lord, and He shall sustain you; He shall never permit the righteous to be moved."

Zechariah 4:6 So he answered and said to me: "This is the word of the Lord to Zerubbabel: 'Not by might nor by power, but by My Spirit,' says the Lord of hosts."

NAMES OF JESUS CHRIST IN THE BIBLE
68) **Rock** (Deuteronomy 32:4),
69) **Root of David** (Revelation 22:16),
70) **Rose of Sharon** (Song of Solomon 2:1),
71) **Sacrifice** (Ephesians 5:2),
72) **Savior** (2 Samuel 22:47; Luke 1:47),
73) **Last Adam** (1 Corinthians 15:45),
74) **Seed of Abraham** (Galatians 3:16),
75) **Seed of David** (2 Timothy 2:8)

For Your Information

FUN FACTS	THE TOP SEVEN POTATO PRODUCING COUNTRIES	TABITHA
1. Abraham Lincoln abolished the slavery in America. 2. Napoleon suffered from ailurophobia which means fear of cats. 3. The purpose of the Bible is to reveal the character of God, His will for mankind. His plan of Salvation for mankind through the Old Testament prophecies about the Messiah and the New Testament arrival of, the ministry and sacrifice of Jesus Christ who rose from the dead and ascended into Heaven until His second coming.	1) China 2) India 3) Russia 4) Ukraine 5) USA 6) Germany 7) Bangladesh	...also known as Dorcas, was a follower of Jesus. When Peter was visiting in Joppa, she died of an unknown cause. Many people mourned her death, for she was loved in the community because of her good works and acts of charity. Peter prayed over her body in the upper room of the house and brought her back to life. As a result, many believed on Jesus.

GROUP DISCUSSION AND CLOSING PRAYER

"Either you run the day, or the day runs you."
Jim Rohn

Day 75 ~ Gaius Status

OPENING PRAYER
READ: 3rd John 1-14

The Elder, To...

1) What was John's prayer for you? _____

_____

2) What type of service should we give to both brethren and the strangers? _____

_____

3) Who are Diotrephes and Demetrius? What does John say about each man? _____

_____

Explore God's World

MEMORY VERSES:

Psalms 55:22 "Cast your burden on the Lord, and He shall sustain you; He shall never permit the righteous to be moved."

Zechariah 4:6 So he answered and said to me: "This is the word of the Lord to Zerubbabel: 'Not by might nor by power, but by My Spirit,' says the Lord of hosts."

NAMES OF JESUS CHRIST IN THE BIBLE
68) **Rock** (Deuteronomy 32:4),
69) **Root of David** (Revelation 22:16),
70) **Rose of Sharon** (Song of Solomon 2:1),
71) **Sacrifice** (Ephesians 5:2),
72) **Savior** (2 Samuel 22:47; Luke 1:47),
73) **Last Adam** (1 Corinthians 15:45),
74) **Seed of Abraham** (Galatians 3:16),
75) **Seed of David** (2 Timothy 2:8)

For Your Information

FUN FACTS	THE TOP SEVEN POTATO PRODUCING COUNTRIES	NAZARITES
1. Rome was founded in the year 753 B.C. 2. Finland won independence in 1917 from Russia. 3. Designed by God, marriage is a "covenant union," not a "contract," between a man and a woman.	1) China 2) India 3) Russia 4) Ukraine 5) USA 6) Germany 7) Bangladesh	...were men, women or slaves who took special, voluntary vows "to separate themselves to the Lord" (Numbers 6:2). The vow included not drinking, not cutting one's hair, and not going near a dead body. Nazarites could take a temporary vow as did the Apostle Paul, but Samson, Samuel, and John the Baptist were the only life-long Nazarites recorded in the Bible. Often times they were dedicated by their parents (although Samson violated all of the vows).

GROUP DISCUSSION AND CLOSING PRAYER

"Life is what happens to you while you're busy making other plans."

John Lennon

Day 76 ~ Warning Against the False Teachers

OPENING PRAYER
READ: Jude 1-12

Jude, a bondservant...

1) Who was Jude and how was he related to Jesus Christ? _____
_____

2) Why did Jude mention Sodom and Gomorrah? _____
_____

3) How have you as a Christian maintained your relationship with God? _____
_____
_____

Explore God's World

MEMORY VERSES:

Psalms 55:22 "Cast your burden on the Lord, and He shall sustain you; He shall never permit the righteous to be moved."

Zechariah 4:6 So he answered and said to me: "This is the word of the Lord to Zerubbabel: 'Not by might nor by power, but by My Spirit,' says the Lord of hosts."

NAMES OF JESUS CHRIST IN THE BIBLE
68) **Rock** (Deuteronomy 32:4),
69) **Root of David** (Revelation 22:16),
70) **Rose of Sharon** (Song of Solomon 2:1),
71) **Sacrifice** (Ephesians 5:2),
72) **Savior** (2 Samuel 22:47; Luke 1:47),
73) **Last Adam** (1 Corinthians 15:45),
74) **Seed of Abraham** (Galatians 3:16),
75) **Seed of David** (2 Timothy 2:8)

For Your Information

FUN FACTS	THE TOP SEVEN POTATO PRODUCING COUNTRIES	THE ALPHA AND OMEGA
1. A standard piano has 88 keys. 2. Montreal, Canada is the second largest French speaking city in the world. 3. There are 30 different types of precious stones mentioned in the Bible.	1) China 2) India 3) Russia 4) Ukraine 5) USA 6) Germany 7) Bangladesh	...are the first and last letters of the Greek alphabet. The expression "the Alpha and the Omega" is used three times in the book of Revelation, referring to God the Father (twice) and the Son (once). The phrase " I am the Alpha and the Omega means "I am the beginning and the end."

GROUP DISCUSSION AND CLOSING PRAYER

"You can never cross the ocean until you have the courage to lose sight of the shore."
Christopher Columbus

Day 77 ~ Week in Review

MEMORIZE AND WRITE

Psalms 55:22 _____

_____

_____

Zechariah 4:6 _____

_____

_____

TRUE OR FALSE — Circle T for true or F for false

T or F   Paul means "honoring God." Timothy was Paul's true son in the faith.

T or F   Finland won independence in 1917 from French.

T or F   Abraham Lincoln was in favor of slavery in America.

T or F   Spain was founded in the year 753 BC.

T or F   Philip was one of the seven deacons chosen to minister to Gentile widows.

T or F   There are 80 different types of precious stones mentioned in the Bible.

T or F   Napoleon suffered from ailurophobia which means fear of spiders.

T or F   A standard piano has 77 keys.

T or F   The sin of simony, or paying for position and influence in the church, is named for Simon.

T or F   Samson, Samuel, and John the Baptist were life-long Nazarites.

MATCH THE FOLLOWING

_____ a. Simon the Sorcerer   1. Covenant union

_____ b. Rome   2. Fear of Cats

_____ c. Montreal   3. 88 keys

_____ d. Abraham Lincoln   4. Russia

_____ e. Precious stones   5. Buy spiritual power

_____ f. Philip   6. Seven deacons

_____ g. Marriage   7. French speaking

_____ h. Napoleon   8. Slavery in America

_____ i. Finland   9. 753 BC

_____ j. Piano   10. Bible

FILL IN THE BLANKS

a. The Alpha and_____ are the_____ and last letters of the_____ alphabet.

b. Designed by_____, marriage is a "_____ _____," not a "contract," between a_____ man and a_____.

c. When Peter was in a_____ town. Tabitha (Dorcas)_____ of an_____ cause

d. Philip was_____ the first_____ to preach outside of_____ (Acts 8).

e. Montreal,_____ is the_____ largest_____ speaking city in the_____.

f. Napoleon_____ from_____ which means_____ of Cats.

g. There are 30_____ types of precious_____ mentioned in the_____.

h. The Nazarite vow included not_____, not cutting_____ _____, and not going near a_____ body.

i. The two most_____ days in your_____ are; the day you are_____ and the day you_____ out why.

j. The_____ of simony, or_____ for position and_____ in the church, is_____ for Simon.

k. Timothy is described as "_____ God" and being Paul's "_____ son in the_____."

LIST THE TOP SEVEN POTATO PRODUCING COUNTRIES

1. _____   2. _____

3. _____   4. _____

5. _____   6. _____

7. _____

CHRISTIAN TESTIMONY

This week shared passages about how we should live and how others see it. Though we live for God's approval, our testimony toward others can be very important to bringing the unsaved to Jesus and encourage the saved to continue living for God. Share some examples where your christian testimony made a difference in someone else. Are there also times where you could have improved your testimony?

_____

_____

_____

_____

_____

Jesus Gives Us Robes of Righteousness Coloring Activity

Note, you may make copies of this page to color if multiple family members in the same household want to color the illustration.

Day 78 ~ Jesus Among the Seven Churches

OPENING PRAYER
READ: Revelation 1:1-20

The Revelation of...

1) Who said, "I am Alpha and Omega, the beginning and the ending"?_____
_____

2) Why was John banished to the Isle of Patmos? _____
_____

3) What are the names of the seven churches?_____
_____

Explore God's World

MEMORY VERSES:

2nd Timothy 3:16-17
"All Scripture is given by inspiration of God, and is profitable for doctrine, for reproof, for correction, for instruction in righteousness, [17] that the man of God may be complete, thoroughly equipped for every good work."

NAMES OF JESUS CHRIST IN THE BIBLE

76) **Seed of the Woman** (Genesis 3:15),
77) **Servant** (Isaiah 42:1),
78) **Shepherd** (1 Peter 2:25),
79) **Shiloh** (Genesis 49:10),
80) **Son of David** (Matthew 15:22),
81) **Son of God** (Luke 1:35),
82) **Son of Man** (Matthew 18:11),
83) **Son of Mary** (Mark 6:3)

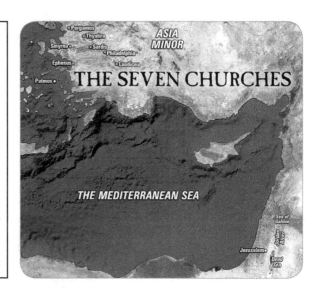

For Your Information

FUN FACTS	THE TOP TEN COUNTRIES WITH THE LOWEST PERCENTAGE OF CHRISTIAN POPULATION	CENSORED CHAPTER
1. In the year 1959, China occupied Tibet. 2. Christopher Columbus died in the year 1506 AD. 3. Jacob had 4 wives, 12 sons and one daughter called Dinah. (Genesis 34:1)	1) Afghanistan 2) Yemen 3) Morocco 4) Maldives 5) Tunisia 6) Turkey 7) Mauritania 8) Algeria 9) Niger 10) Somalia	...The first chapter of Ezekiel may have portrayed God's majesty, but it was so strange to Jewish priests that Jewish young people under 30 years old were not allowed to read it.

GROUP DISCUSSION AND CLOSING PRAYER

"It takes 20 years to build a reputation and five minutes to ruin it."
Warren Buffett

Day 79 ~ The Letters to the Seven Churches

OPENING PRAYER

READ: Revelation 2:1-23 and 3:22

To the angel...

1) What were the conditions of the churches in Ephesus, Smyrna, and Pergamos?_____
_____

2) What can you learn from the churches of Thyatira, Sardis, Philadelphia, and Laodicea? _____
_____

3) Which of the seven churches do you identify with your church?_____
_____

Explore God's World

MEMORY VERSES:

2nd Timothy 3:16-17 "All Scripture is given by inspiration of God, and is profitable for doctrine, for reproof, for correction, for instruction in righteousness, [17] that the man of God may be complete, thoroughly equipped for every good work."

NAMES OF JESUS CHRIST IN THE BIBLE
76) **Seed of the Woman** (Genesis 3:15),
77) **Servant** (Isaiah 42:1),
78) **Shepherd** (1 Peter 2:25),
79) **Shiloh** (Genesis 49:10),
80) **Son of David** (Matthew 15:22),
81) **Son of God** (Luke 1:35),
82) **Son of Man** (Matthew 18:11),
83) **Son of Mary** (Mark 6:3)

For Your Information

FUN FACTS	THE TOP TEN COUNTRIES WITH THE LOWEST PERCENTAGE OF CHRISTIAN POPULATION	PROVERBS
1. The headquarters of the United Nations is in New York, NY. 2. Covering 13000 square miles, Wrangell-St. Elias National Park in Alaska is the largest park in the USA. 3. Shadrach, Meshach, and Abednego were thrown into the furnace for not bowing to King Nebuchadnezzar, but the fire did not harm them.	1) Afghanistan 2) Yemen 3) Morocco 4) Maldives 5) Tunisia 6) Turkey 7) Mauritania 8) Algeria 9) Niger 10) Somalia	...is one of the most practical books in the Bible because of its Godly common-sense approach to life. The wisdom is captured in hundreds of short, pithy sayings about how to live life well with God and our neighbors.

GROUP DISCUSSION AND CLOSING PRAYER

"Our ability to have patience, and our attitude toward others, define who we are at any given time"

Ellen J. Barrier

Day 80 ~ The Throne, the Scroll, and the Lamb

OPENING PRAYER

READ: Revelation 4:1-8 and 5:1-14

After these things...

1) Whose throne did John see and how many lamps were there?_____
_____

2) What did a strong angel proclaim with a loud voice? What made John weep?_____
_____

3) What is said in 5:12? Who does the Lamb represent?_____
_____
_____

Explore God's World

MEMORY VERSES:

2nd Timothy 3:16-17 "All Scripture is given by inspiration of God, and is profitable for doctrine, for reproof, for correction, for instruction in righteousness, [17] that the man of God may be complete, thoroughly equipped for every good work."

NAMES OF JESUS CHRIST IN THE BIBLE
76) **Seed of the Woman** (Genesis 3:15),
77) **Servant** (Isaiah 42:1),
78) **Shepherd** (1 Peter 2:25),
79) **Shiloh** (Genesis 49:10),
80) **Son of David** (Matthew 15:22),
81) **Son of God** (Luke 1:35),
82) **Son of Man** (Matthew 18:11),
83) **Son of Mary** (Mark 6:3)

For Your Information

FUN FACTS	THE TOP TEN COUNTRIES WITH THE LOWEST PERCENTAGE OF CHRISTIAN POPULATION	ECCLESIASTES
1. Venice is also known as the City of Canals. 2. Portugal leads the world in the production of cork. 3. When Queen Vashti refused to honor King Xerxes, he became furious and banished her. Esther was chosen from among the beautiful maidens of the land to succeed her as queen.	1) Afghanistan 2) Yemen 3) Morocco 4) Maldives 5) Tunisia 6) Turkey 7) Mauritania 8) Algeria 9) Niger 10) Somalia	...was written by an unnamed writer who had tried everything "under the sun" to find meaning in life, but only experienced frustration and cynicism. The author concluded the book by affirming that life has meaning when one lives in a right relationship with God. The book is the closest Biblical writing to what the Greeks called "philosophy".

GROUP DISCUSSION AND CLOSING PRAYER

"Patience and wisdom walk hand in hand, like two one-armed lovers."
Jarod Kintz

Day 81 ~ The Seven Seals

OPENING PRAYER

READ: Revelation 6:1-17 and 8:1-8

Now I saw...

1) Which seal speaks about the cry of the martyrs?_____
_____

2) Name the seven seals and briefly explain the 7th seal._____
_____

3) Name the tribes?_____
_____

Explore God's World

MEMORY VERSES:

2nd Timothy 3:16-17 "All Scripture is given by inspiration of God, and is profitable for doctrine, for reproof, for correction, for instruction in righteousness, [17] that the man of God may be complete, thoroughly equipped for every good work."

NAMES OF JESUS CHRIST IN THE BIBLE

76) **Seed of the Woman** (Genesis 3:15),
77) **Servant** (Isaiah 42:1),
78) **Shepherd** (1 Peter 2:25),
79) **Shiloh** (Genesis 49:10),
80) **Son of David** (Matthew 15:22),
81) **Son of God** (Luke 1:35),
82) **Son of Man** (Matthew 18:11),
83) **Son of Mary** (Mark 6:3)

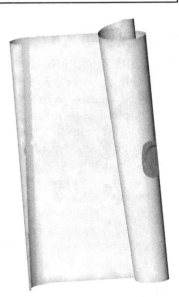

For Your Information

FUN FACTS	THE TOP TEN COUNTRIES WITH THE LOWEST PERCENTAGE OF CHRISTIAN POPULATION	ANCIENT WORDS OF WORSHIP
1. In the year 1959, China occupied Tibet. 2. Christopher Columbus died in the year 1506 AD. 3. Jacob had 4 wives, 12 sons and one daughter called Dinah. (Genesis 34:1)	1) *Afghanistan* 2) *Yemen* 3) *Morocco* 4) *Maldives* 5) *Tunisia* 6) *Turkey* 7) *Mauritania* 8) *Algeria* 9) *Niger* 10) *Somalia*	...are used in modern-day worship. Hallelujah is Hebrew for "Praise the Lord!" Hosanna, a Hebrew derivative originally meaning "Save us," was a shout of acclamation used to welcome Jesus into Jerusalem. Amen is Hebrew for "Surely! So be it!" Maranatha is an Aramaic word used by Paul meaning "Our Lord, come!" (referring to hopes of Christ's return to earth.)

GROUP DISCUSSION AND CLOSING PRAYER

"Face reality as it is, not as it was or as you wish it to be."
Jack Welch

Day 82 ~ The Seven Trumpets

OPENING PRAYER

READ: Revelation 8:2-13 and 9:21

And I saw...

1) What happened when the angel took the censer, filled it with fire from the altar, and threw it?____
_____

2) List the first six trumpets. What happened to the water? _____
_____

3) What was the 5th trumpet and how were the locusts described?_____
_____

Explore God's World

MEMORY VERSES:
2nd Timothy 3:16-17
"All Scripture is given by inspiration of God, and is profitable for doctrine, for reproof, for correction, for instruction in righteousness, [17] that the man of God may be complete, thoroughly equipped for every good work."

NAMES OF JESUS CHRIST IN THE BIBLE
76) **Seed of the Woman** (Genesis 3:15),
77) **Servant** (Isaiah 42:1),
78) **Shepherd** (1 Peter 2:25),
79) **Shiloh** (Genesis 49:10),
80) **Son of David** (Matthew 15:22),
81) **Son of God** (Luke 1:35),
82) **Son of Man** (Matthew 18:11),
83) **Son of Mary** (Mark 6:3)

For Your Information

FUN FACTS
1. The headquarters of the United Nations is in New York, NY.
2. Covering 13000 square miles, Wrangell-St. Elias National Park in Alaska is the largest park in the USA.
3. Shadrach, Meshach, and Abednego were thrown into the furnace for not bowing to King Nebuchadnezzar, but the fire did not harm them.

THE TOP TEN COUNTRIES WITH THE LOWEST PERCENTAGE OF CHRISTIAN POPULATION
1) Afghanistan 2) Yemen
3) Morocco 4) Maldives
5) Tunisia 6) Turkey
7) Mauritania 8) Algeria
9) Niger 10) Somalia

THE LANGUAGE OF JESUS
...was Aramaic, which is closely related to Hebrew. The language all but died out in the centuries following Jesus' day. Amazingly, the language survives today only in isolated villages in Syria, Turkey, Iraq, and Iran. Assyrian Christians from northern Iraq speak Aramaic today.

GROUP DISCUSSION AND CLOSING PRAYER

"If you are irritated by every rub, how will your mirror be polished."
Rumi

Day 83 ~ *The Seven Trumpets*

OPENING PRAYER

READ: Revelation 10:1-11 and 11:1-19

I saw still...

1) What was given to John by the angel and what did he do with it? _____

_____

2) Why and by whom were the two witnesses killed? _____

_____

3) What was the 7th trumpet? How many elders were there? _____

_____

_____

Explore God's World

MEMORY VERSES:

2nd Timothy 3:16-17 "All Scripture is given by inspiration of God, and is profitable for doctrine, for reproof, for correction, for instruction in righteousness, [17] that the man of God may be complete, thoroughly equipped for every good work."

NAMES OF JESUS CHRIST IN THE BIBLE
76) **Seed of the Woman** (Genesis 3:15),
77) **Servant** (Isaiah 42:1),
78) **Shepherd** (1 Peter 2:25),
79) **Shiloh** (Genesis 49:10),
80) **Son of David** (Matthew 15:22),
81) **Son of God** (Luke 1:35),
82) **Son of Man** (Matthew 18:11),
83) **Son of Mary** (Mark 6:3)

For Your Information

FUN FACTS	THE TOP TEN COUNTRIES WITH THE LOWEST PERCENTAGE OF CHRISTIAN POPULATION	THE MOST GENEROUS PERSON IN THE BIBLE
1. Venice is also known as the City of Canals. 2. Portugal leads the world in the production of cork. 3. When Queen Vashti refused to honor King Xerxes, he became furious and banished her. Esther was chosen from among the beautiful maidens of the land to succeed her as queen.	*1) Afghanistan 2) Yemen 3) Morocco 4) Maldives 5) Tunisia 6) Turkey 7) Mauritania 8) Algeria 9) Niger 10) Somalia*	...is the poor widow whom Jesus saw dropping two small copper coins into the treasury box in the Temple. These were the least valuable coins in circulation (less than a penny) and yet, they were the only money she owned. Thus, she gave "all she had to live on." (Mark 12:44)

GROUP DISCUSSION AND CLOSING PRAYER

"The only true wisdom is in knowing you know nothing."
Socrates

Day 84 ~ Week in Review

MATCH THE FOLLOWING

_____ a. Maranatha		1. Greeks-philosophy
_____ b. Headquarters		2. Dinah
_____ c. Aramaic speaking		3. Practical books
_____ d. Christopher Columbus		4. Syria, Turkey, Iraq, and Iran
_____ e. King Xerxes		5. Our Lord, come
_____ f. Censored Chapter		6. United Nations
_____ g. Ecclesiastes		7. 1506 AD
_____ h. Jacob		8. Esther
_____ i. Proverbs		9. Ezekiel

TRUE OR FALSE — Circle T for true or F for false

T or F   Queen Vashti refused to honor King Xerxes.

T or F   Christopher Columbus died in the year 1956 AD.

T or F   The headquarters of the United Nations is in Dubai, UAE.

T or F   Philemon is one of the most practical books in the Bible.

T or F   Wrangell-St. Elias National Park in AK is the smallest park in the USA.

T or F   In the year 1959, Japan occupied Korea.

T or F   Madrid is also known as the City of Canals.

T or F   Jacob had 5 wives,17 sons, and one daughter called Dinah.

LIST THE TOP TEN COUNTRIES WITH THE LOWEST PERCENTAGE OF CHRISTIAN POPULATION

1. _____   2. _____

3. _____   4. _____

5. _____   6. _____

7. _____   8. _____

9. _____   10. _____

FILL IN THE BLANKS

a. Jacob had 4 wives, 12 _____, and one _____ called Dinah. (_____ 34:1).

b. Covering _____sq miles, Wrangell-St. _____ National Park in Alaska is the _____ park in the_____.

c. Portugal leads the_____in the production of _____.

d. Shadrach,_____, and _____were thrown into the _____for not bowing to King _____, but the fire did not _____them.

e. Proverbs is one of the most _____books in the _____ because of its_____common-sense _____to life.

f. The Language of _____ was Aramaic, which is_____ related to _____.

g. When_____Vashti refused to honor King _____, he became_____and banished her.

h. Maranatha is an _____word used by _____ meaning "Our _____, come!"

MEMORIZE AND WRITE

2nd Timothy 3:16-17 _____

_____

_____

_____

WRITE AND MEMORIZE DIFFERENT NAMES OF JESUS CHRIST FOUND IN THE BIBLE

1. _____   2. _____

3. _____   4. _____

5. _____   6. _____

7. _____   8. _____

THE PRESENCE OF JESUS CHRIST

At the beginning of Revelation, Jesus is seen in the midst of the churches. Just like that, He is in the midst of us, the Church, His believers. How can you better acknowledge and live like Jesus is present with you?

_____

_____

_____

FAMILY PROJECT

Find something this week where you can share the love of God to someone else and be a testimony.

Day 85 ~ The Woman, the Child and the Dragon

OPENING PRAYER
READ: Revelation 12:1-17

Now a great...

1) Describe the dragon. What does he do to the Child? _____

_____

2) With whom do Michael and his angels fight? Who prevailed? _____

_____

3) What happened to the woman? What does she do with the two wings? _____

_____

Explore God's World

MEMORY VERSES:

Revelation 22:18-19 "For I testify to everyone who ears the words of the prophecy of this book: If anyone adds to these things, God will add to him the plagues that are written in this book; [19] and if anyone takes away from the words of the book of this prophecy, God shall take away his part from the Book of Life, from the Holy City, and from the things which are written in this book."

NAMES OF JESUS CHRIST IN THE BIBLE
84) **Son of the Most High** (Luke 1:32),
85) **Cornerstone** (Isaiah 28:16),
86) **Sun of Righteousness** (Malachi 4:2),
87) **Teacher** (Matthew 26:18),
88) **Truth** (John 14:6),
89) **Way** (John 14:6),
90) **Wonderful Counselor** (Isaiah 9:6),
91) **Word** (John 1:1),
92) **Vine** (John 15:1)

For Your Information

FUN FACTS

1. Japan is called the Land of the Rising Sun.
2. The Red Cross was founded by Jean Henri Durant, a Swiss business-man and social activist.
3. Lot's wife turned into a pillar of salt after she looked back at the destruction of Sodom and Gomorrah.

THE SEVEN LARGEST SHOPPING MALLS IN THE WORLD

1) **New South China Mall**, *China*
2) **Golden Resources Mall**, *China*
3) **SM City North EDSA**, *Philippines*
4) **SM Megamall**, *Philippines*
5) **Isfahan City Center**, *Iran*
6) **1Utama**, *Malaysia*
7) **Persian Gulf Complex**, *Iran*

MUSTARD SEED

…is mentioned as the smallest seed in the Bible. The plant grows close to five feet tall. Jesus used it to characterize the growth of God's kingdom, from something small (the tiny seed) to something great (the large plant), as well as to speak of the tiny amount of faith needed to work wonders.

GROUP DISCUSSION AND CLOSING PRAYER

"In the end, it's not the years in your life that counts. It's the life in your years."

Abraham Lincoln

Day 86 ~ The Two Beasts

OPENING PRAYER

READ: Revelation 13:1-18

Then I stood...

1) Where does the beast come from? Describe the beast. _____

_____

2) What do you learn from verses 7 and 8? _____

_____

3) Describe the second beast which came out of the earth? _____

_____

Explore God's World

Revelation 22:18-19 "For I testify to everyone who ears the words of the prophecy of this book: If anyone adds to these things, God will add to him the plagues that are written in this book; [19] and if anyone takes away from the words of the book of this prophecy, God shall take away his part from the Book of Life, from the Holy City, and from the things which are written in this book."

NAMES OF JESUS CHRIST IN THE BIBLE
84) **Son of the Most High** (Luke 1:32),
85) **Cornerstone** (Isaiah 28:16),
86) **Sun of Righteousness** (Malachi 4:2),
87) **Teacher** (Matthew 26:18),
88) **Truth** (John 14:6),
89) **Way** (John 14:6),
90) **Wonderful Counselor** (Isaiah 9:6),
91) **Word** (John 1:1),
92) **Vine** (John 15:1)

For Your Information

FUN FACTS	THE SEVEN LARGEST SHOPPING MALLS IN THE WORLD	IMMANUEL
1. Arthur Wynney invented the crossword puzzle. 2. Bahrain is the only country whose national anthem has music, but no words. 3. In exile, Daniel prayed three times a day in his upper room, where the windows opened toward Jerusalem.	1) **New South China Mall**, *China* 2) **Golden Resources Mall**, *China* 3) **SM City North EDSA**, *Philippines* 4) **SM Megamall**, *Philippines* 5) **Isfahan City Center**, *Iran* 6) **1Utama**, *Malaysia* 7) **Persian Gulf Complex**, *Iran*	...is the name given to the Messiah whose birth was foretold in the Old Testament. Isaiah 7:14, one of the most famous prophecies about the promised Anointed One, states that a virgin will conceive and bear a son named Immanuel. This name is Imma-nu-el in Hebrew, literally translated as "with us (is) God." Matthew 1:23 quotes this prophecy as having been fulfilled in Jesus.

GROUP DISCUSSION AND CLOSING PRAYER

"I am not a product of my circumstances. I am a product of my decisions."

Stephens Convey

Day 87 ~ The Lamb, the 144,000, & the Harvest of the Earth

OPENING PRAYER

READ: Revelation 14:1-20

Then I looked,...

1) What voice did John hear from heaven? _____
_____

2) What was the message the three angels proclaimed? _____
_____

3) What power did the angel carrying the sharp sickle have?_____
_____

Explore God's World

MEMORY VERSES:

Revelation 22:18-19 "For I testify to everyone who ears the words of the prophecy of this book: If anyone adds to these things, God will add to him the plagues that are written in this book; [19] and if anyone takes away from the words of the book of this prophecy, God shall take away his part from the Book of Life, from the Holy City, and from the things which are written in this book."

NAMES OF JESUS CHRIST IN THE BIBLE

84) **Son of the Most High** (Luke 1:32),
85) **Cornerstone** (Isaiah 28:16),
86) **Sun of Righteousness** (Malachi 4:2),
87) **Teacher** (Matthew 26:18),
88) **Truth** (John 14:6),
89) **Way** (John 14:6),
90) **Wonderful Counselor** (Isaiah 9:6),
91) **Word** (John 1:1),
92) **Vine** (John 15:1)

For Your Information

FUN FACTS	THE SEVEN LARGEST SHOPPING MALLS IN THE WORLD	I.N.R.I.
1. Pen is the name given to the female swan. 2. Butterflies have six legs, and a baby seal is called a pup. 3. It was King Nebuchadnezzar who ate grass like the oxen for seven years. (Daniel 4:33).	1) **New South China Mall**, *China* 2) **Golden Resources Mall**, *China* 3) **SM City North EDSA**, *Philippines* 4) **SM Megamall**, *Philippines* 5) **Isfahan City Center**, *Iran* 6) **1Utama**, *Malaysia* 7) **Persian Gulf Complex**, *Iran*	...are the letters often seen on the plaque in paintings of Jesus' crucifixion. The letters represent the Latin words for "Jesus of Nazareth, King of the Jews". The four Gospels state that this identity of Jesus was written in Hebrew, Latin, and Greek.

GROUP DISCUSSION AND CLOSING PRAYER

"Don't try to rush things: for the cup to run over, it must first be filled."

Antonio Machado

Day 88 ~ The Seven Bowls

OPENING PRAYER

READ: Revelation 15:1-8 and 16:1-21

Then I saw...

1) What song were the victorious saints singing?_____

_____

2) What did one of the living creatures give to the seven angels? Name the seven bowls._____

_____

3) What did John see coming out of the mouths of the dragon, the beast, and the false prophet?____

_____

Explore God's World

MEMORY VERSES:

Revelation 22:18-19 "For I testify to everyone who ears the words of the prophecy of this book: If anyone adds to these things, God will add to him the plagues that are written in this book; ¹⁹ and if anyone takes away from the words of the book of this prophecy, God shall take away his part from the Book of Life, from the Holy City, and from the things which are written in this book."

NAMES OF JESUS CHRIST IN THE BIBLE
84) **Son of the Most High** (Luke 1:32),
85) **Cornerstone** (Isaiah 28:16),
86) **Sun of Righteousness** (Malachi 4:2),
87) **Teacher** (Matthew 26:18),
88) **Truth** (John 14:6),
89) **Way** (John 14:6),
90) **Wonderful Counselor** (Isaiah 9:6),
91) **Word** (John 1:1),
92) **Vine** (John 15:1)

For Your Information

FUN FACTS	THE SEVEN LARGEST SHOPPING MALLS IN THE WORLD	A SECRET PASSWORD
1. Japan is called the Land of the Rising Sun. 2. The Red Cross was founded by Jean Henri Durant, a Swiss businessman and social activist. 3. Lot's wife turned into a pillar of salt after she looked back at the destruction of Sodom and Gomorrah.	1) **New South China Mall**, *China* 2) **Golden Resources Mall**, *China* 3) **SM City North EDSA**, *Philippines* 4) **SM Megamall**, *Philippines* 5) **Isfahan City Center**, *Iran* 6) **1Utama**, *Malaysia* 7) **Persian Gulf Complex**, *Iran*	...used by the early Christians was the symbol of the fish written as graffiti because they were being persecuted by the Romans. The Greek word for fish, "Ichthus," is an acronym for the Greek phrase, "Iesous Christos Theou Uios Soter," or "Jesus Christ the Son of God, Saviour."

GROUP DISCUSSION AND CLOSING PRAYER

"Every saint has a past, and every sinner has a future."

Oscar Wilde

Day 89 ~ The Wedding of the Lamb and 1000 Years

After these things...

OPENING PRAYER

READ: Revelation 19:1-16 and 20:1-15

1) Who was on the White Horse? What was He called? What does He do? _____

_____

2) What do you learn from 20:4? Who will reign with Christ? _____

_____

3) What does the great white throne represent ? How are the dead judged?_____

_____

Explore God's World

MEMORY VERSES:

Revelation 22:18-19 "For I testify to everyone who ears the words of the prophecy of this book: If anyone adds to these things, God will add to him the plagues that are written in this book; [19] and if anyone takes away from the words of the book of this prophecy, God shall take away his part from the Book of Life, from the Holy City, and from the things which are written in this book."

NAMES OF JESUS CHRIST IN THE BIBLE
84) **Son of the Most High** (Luke 1:32),
85) **Cornerstone** (Isaiah 28:16),
86) **Sun of Righteousness** (Malachi 4:2),
87) **Teacher** (Matthew 26:18),
88) **Truth** (John 14:6),
89) **Way** (John 14:6),
90) **Wonderful Counselor** (Isaiah 9:6),
91) **Word** (John 1:1),
92) **Vine** (John 15:1)

For Your Information

FUN FACTS	THE SEVEN LARGEST SHOPPING MALLS IN THE WORLD	THE MOST EXPENSIVE BIBLE
1. Arthur Wynney invented the crossword puzzle. 2. Bahrain is the only country whose national anthem has music, but no words. 3. In exile, Daniel prayed three times a day in his upper room, where the windows opened toward Jerusalem.	1) **New South China Mall**, *China* 2) **Golden Resources Mall**, *China* 3) **SM City North EDSA**, *Philippines* 4) **SM Megamall**, *Philippines* 5) **Isfahan City Center**, *Iran* 6) **1Utama**, *Malaysia* 7) **Persian Gulf Complex**, *Iran*	...ever purchased is the copy of Gutenberg's Old Testament containing Genesis through Psalms printed in 1455 A.D. On October 22, 1987, this bible sold for $5.39 million at a Christie's auction in New York.

GROUP DISCUSSION AND CLOSING PRAYER

"Peace is a product of both patience and persistence."

Camron Wright

Day 90 ~ New Heaven, New Earth, New Jerusalem
Then one of...

OPENING PRAYER
READ: Revelation 21:9-27 and 22:1-19

1) How do you describe the glory of the New Jerusalem? _____
_____

2) What does the pure river of water of life represent, and how will it bless the believers? _____
_____

3) What will God do with anyone who adds to or takes away from the book of prophecy? _____
_____

Explore God's World

MEMORY VERSES:

Revelation 22:18-19 "For I testify to everyone who ears the words of the prophecy of this book: If anyone adds to these things, God will add to him the plagues that are written in this book; [19] and if anyone takes away from the words of the book of this prophecy, God shall take away his part from the Book of Life, from the Holy City, and from the things which are written in this book."

NAMES OF JESUS CHRIST IN THE BIBLE
84) **Son of the Most High** (Luke 1:32),
85) **Cornerstone** (Isaiah 28:16),
86) **Sun of Righteousness** (Malachi 4:2),
87) **Teacher** (Matthew 26:18),
88) **Truth** (John 14:6),
89) **Way** (John 14:6),
90) **Wonderful Counselor** (Isaiah 9:6),
91) **Word** (John 1:1),
92) **Vine** (John 15:1)

For Your Information

FUN FACTS	THE SEVEN LARGEST SHOPPING MALLS IN THE WORLD	THE GOLDEN RULE
1. Pen is the name given to the female swan. 2. Butterflies have six legs, and a baby seal is called a pup. 3. It was King Nebuchadnezzar who ate grass like the oxen for seven years. (Daniel 4:33).	1) **New South China Mall**, *China* 2) **Golden Resources Mall**, *China* 3) **SM City North EDSA**, *Philippines* 4) **SM Megamall**, *Philippines* 5) **Isfahan City Center**, *Iran* 6) **1Utama**, *Malaysia* 7) **Persian Gulf Complex**, *Iran*	...is summarized by Jesus, who reduced the entire Law of Moses to "You shall love the Lord your God with all your heart, soul, and mind, and love your neighbor as yourself." (Matthew 22:37-40) Jesus was quoting Deuteronomy 6:5 and Leviticus 19:18.

GROUP DISCUSSION AND CLOSING PRAYER

"I have decided to stick with love. Hate is too great a burden to bear."

Martin Luther King Jr.

Day 91 ~ Week in Review

MEMORIZE AND WRITE

Revelation 22:18-19 _____

_____

_____

TRUE OR FALSE — Circle T for true or F for false

T or F   The fish was a symbol of the early persecuted Christians' secret password.

T or F   Butterflies have 8 legs, and a baby seal is called a pup.

T or F   The Red Cross was founded by Steve Henri Pasquet, a Swiss priest and poet.

T or F   Penny is the name given to the female swan.

T or F   The name Immanuel is the most famous prophecy about the Messiah in the whole Bible.

T or F   It was King Nebuchadnezzar who ate grass like the oxen.

T or F   All four Gospels state that INRI was written on a plague placed in Jesus' cross to identify Him.

T or F   Bahrain is the only country whose national anthem has music but no words.

MATCH THE FOLLOWING

_____ a. Daniel   1. Sir Robert Walpole

_____ b. Arthur Wynney   2. Sir Thomas Stamford Raffles

_____ c. Japan   3. China

_____ d. Immanuel   4. David Ben-Gurian

_____ e. Bahrain   5. Leah and Rachel

_____ f. Swan   6. Egypt

_____ g. Lot   7. Soviet Union

_____ h. The Red Cross   8. With us (is) God

_____ i. Mustard Seed   9. Jean Henri Durant

WRITE THE SEVEN LARGEST SHOPPING MALLS IN THE WORLD

1. _____   2. _____

3. _____   4. _____

5. _____   6. _____

7. _____

FILL IN THE BLANKS

a. The Red _____ was founded by Jean Henri _____ , a Swiss _____ and social _____ .

b. Imma-nu-el in _____ literally translated means "_____ us (is) _____ ".

c. Butterflies have 6 _____ and _____ seal is called a _____ .

d. Bahrain is the only _____ whose national _____ has music but no _____ .

e. The most expensive bible ever purchased is the copy of _____ Old Testament containing Genesis through _____ .

f. It was King _____ who ate grass like the oxen for _____ years. (_____ 4:33).

LIST THE NAMES OF JESUS CHRIST IN THE BOOK OF REVELATION

1. _____   2. _____

3. _____   4. _____

5. _____   6. _____

7. _____   8. _____

9. _____

OUR HOPE

As you just read this week our greatest hope when history ends and eternity begins. But our hope does not start at the end. Jesus has promised an abundant life now even while we still deal with the effects of a sinful world. Discuss and write down how you can see the believer's hope now.

_____

_____

_____

_____

_____

_____

_____

_____

_____

Jesus Is the White Rider Coloring Activity

Note, you may make copies of this page to color if multiple family members in the same household want to color the illustration.

GLOSSARY & REFERENCES

A

Abbreviated—[uh-bree-vee-ey-tid] To shorten or reduce (anything) in length.

Aboriginal—[ab-uh-rij-uh-nl] Original or earliest known; native; indigenous.

Accumulation—[uh-kyoo-myuh-ley-shuh n] Something that has been collected, gathered.

Admonished—[ad-mon-ish] To caution, advise, or counsel against something.

Ancient—Dating from a remote period; of great age.

Adulterous—Unfaithful

Alleviate—[uh-lee-vee-eyt] lighten, easier to bear, relieve.

Anonymous—uh-non-uh-muh s] Without any name acknowledged, as that of author or Contributor.

Apocalyptic—[uh-pok-uh-lip-tik] Predicting an imminent disaster or universal destruction.

Apokalupsis—[uh-pok-uh-lips] Any revelation or prophecy.

Apostolic—[ap-uh-stol-ik] Pertaining to or characteristic of the 12 Apostles.

Archipelago—[ahr-kuh-pel-uh-goh] Any large body of water with many islands.

Asceticism—[uh-set-uh-siz uh m] The doctrine that a person can attain a high spiritual and moral state by practicing self-denial, self-mortification, and the like.

Asymmetrical—[ey-suh-me-trik, as-uh-] not identical on both sides of a central line, unsymmetrical.

Atonement—The reconciliation of man with God through the life, sufferings, and sacrificial death of Jesus Christ

Atrocities—[uh-tros-i-tee] Behaviour or an action that is wicked or ruthless.

Autobiographical—Marked by or dealing with one's own experiences or life history.

Autopsy—[aw-top-see] inspection of a body after death, as for determination of the cause of death.

B

Beethoven—German composer (1770–1827)

Beetle—Any of various insects resembling the beetle, as a cockroach.

Bosom—The breast of a human being.

Botany—The branch of biology that deals with plant life.

C

Camouflage—[kam-uh-flahzh] As by painting or screening objects so that they are lost lost to view in thebackground.

Cannibals—Any animal that eats its own kind.

Cays—A small low Island

Cerinthianism—A heresy taught that deals with the person of Jesus.

Cessation—[se-sey-shuh n] a temporary or complete stopping; discontinuance.

Chronicles—A record or register of events in chronological order

Chronological—A sequence of events, arranged in order of occurrence.

Circumcision—The rite of circumcising, spiritual purification.

Circumspect—[sur-*kuh* m-spekt] watchful and discreet; cautious; prudent.

Colosseum—An ancient amphitheater in Rome, begun AD 70.

Commencement—[*kuh*-mens-*muh* nt] To Begin.

Compulsory—[*kuh* m-puhl-*suh*-ree] Required; mandatory; obligatory.

Conclusive—[*kuh* n-kloo-siv] Serving to settle or decide a question; decisive; convincing.

Condemnation—[kon-dem-ney-sh*uh* n, -*duh* m-] To pronounce to be guilty, sentence to punishment.

Contemplating—To consider thoroughly.

Contending—To struggle in opposition:

Continent—The mainland, as distinguished from islands or peninsulas.

Conservation—[kon-ser-vey-sh*uh* n] The careful utilization of a natural resource in order to prevent depletion.

Consistent—[*kuh* n-sis-t*uh* nt] Agreeing or accordant; compatible; not self-contradictory.

Conspiracy—[*kuh* n-spir-*uh*-see] A combination of persons for a secret, unlawful or evil purpose.

Cortex—The outer region of an organ or structure, as theouter portion of the kidney.

Covenant—An oath or agreement, deed.

Cumulative—[kyoo-my*uh-luh*-tiv, -ley-tiv] growing in quantity, strength, or effect.

Cymbals—[sim bah l] A concave plate of brass or bronze that produces a sharp, ringing sound when struck.

D

Decay—To decline in excellence, prosperity, health, etc.

Deforestation—The cutting down and removal of all or most of thetrees in a forested area.

Decimated—[des-*uh*-meyt] To destroy or kill a large proportion of: *a plague.*

Deities—A god or goddess.

Delicacy—[del-i-*kuh*-see] something delightful or pleasing, especially a choice considered with regard to its rarity.

Depravity—To make morally bad or evil; vitiate; corrupt.

Deliverance—To set free or release.

Deportation—The lawful expulsion of an undesired alien or otherperson from a state.

Descendants—A person or animal that is descended from aspecific ancestor; an offspring.

Desertification—[dih-zur-t*uh*-fi-key-sh*uh* n] A process by which fertile land turns into barren land or desert.

Detection—To discover or catch (a person) in the performance of some act.

Derived—To trace from a source or origin.

Deuteronomy—[doo-*tuh*-ron-*uh*-mee, dyoo-] The 5th book in the Bible.

Dictatorial—Appropriate to, or characteristic of, a dictator; absolute; unlimited: dictatorial power in wartime.

Differentiate—To form or mark differently from other such things; distinguish.

Diligently—Constant in effort to accomplish something.

Diotrephes—A man mentioned in the Third Epistle of John (verses 9–11). His name means "nourished by Jupiter."

Disciplinary—Training to act in accordance with rules; drill.

Distorted—[dih-stawr-tid] not truly or completely representing the facts or reality; misrepresented; false.

Docetism—[doh-see-tiz-*uh* m, doh-si-tiz] A early Christian doctrine that the sufferings of Christ were apparent and not real and that after the crucifixion He appeared in a spiritual body.

Doctrines—A particular principle, position, or policy taught oradvocated, as of a religion or government.

Drought—A period of dry weather, especially a long one that is injurious to crops.

E

Ecclesiastes—[ih-klee-zee-as-teez] A book of the Bible.

Economy—thrifty management; thoughtful or wise in spending resources.

Elixirs—[ih-lik-ser] A sweetened aromatic solution of alcohol and water serving as a vehicle for medicine.

Elohim—[e-loh-him] God, especially as used in the Hebrew text of the Old Testament.

Emerges—To rise or come forth from or as if from water or other liquid.

Emphasis—Something that is given great stress or importance.

Ensues—To follow in order; come afterward, especially in immediate succession.

Entrepreneur—[ahn-truh-pruh-nur] A person who organizes and manages any enterprise, especially a business.

Epistle—A letter, especially a formal or instructive one.

Exaltation—Raise or elevate, as in rank or character; of high station.

Exclusion—[ik-skloo-zhuh n] To shut or keep out; prevent the entrance of.

Exodus—A going out; a departure or emigration, usually of a large number of people.

Exile—To expel or banish (a person) from his or her country.

Explicitly—Precisely and clearly expressed, leaving nothing to implication; fully stated.

Exporter—To ship (commodities) to other countries or places for sale, exchange, etc.

F

Fending off—To try to prevent something.

Forensic—[fuh-ren-sik] The art or study of argumentation and formal debate.

Forewarned—[fawr-wawrn, foh] To warn in advance.

Francophone—[frang-kuh-fohn] A person who speaks French, especially a native speak.

Frenzied—[fren-zeed] Wildly excited or enthusiastic.

Frontlets—[fruhnt-lit] A decorative band, ribbon, or the like, worn across the forehead.

Futility—[fyoo-til-i-tee] The quality of being futile; ineffectiveness; uselessness.

G

Genealogical—[jee-nee-ol-uh-jee, -al-, jen-ee-] A record or account of the ancestry and descent of a person, family, group, etc.

Gentile—[jen-tahyl] A person who is not Jewish, especially a Christian.

Genres—A class or category of artistic endeavor having a particular form, content, technique, or the like the genre of epic poetry; the genre of symphonic music.

GDP—Gross domestic product.

Gnostic—[nos-tik] Pertaining to knowledge.

H

Hedonism—[heed-n-iz-uh m] the doctrine that pleasure or happiness is the highest good.

Heresy—[her-uh-see] Opinion or doctrine at variance with the orthodox or accepted doctrine, especially of a church or religious system.

Holocaust—[hol-uh-kawst] A great or complete devastation or destruction, especially by fire.

Hymnal—[him-nl] A book of hymns/songs for use in a religious service.

Hypocrites—[hip-uh-krit] A person who pretends to have virtues, moral or religious beliefs, priniciples.

I

Idolatrous—[ahy-dol-uh-truh s] Worshiping idols.

IMF—The International Monetary Fund.

Immense—Vast; huge; very great

Immorality—[im-*uh*-ral-i-tee] Immoral character, or conduct; wickedness; evilness.

Impending—About to happen; imminent.

Importer—To bring in (merchandise, commodities, workers,etc.) from a foreign country for use, sale,processing, reexport, or services.

Imputation—[im-pyoo-tey-sh*uh* n] An attribution, as of fault or crime; accusation.

Indigenous—[in-dij-*uh*-n*uh* s] Originating in and characteristic of a particular region or country; native.

Inevitable—[in-ev-i-t*uh*-b*uh* l] Unable to be avoided, evaded, or escaped; certain; necessary.

Ingredient—[in-gree-dee-*uh* nt]Something that enters as an element into a mixture.

Inhabitants—[nˈhæb ɪ tənt/] A person or animal that inhabits a place, especially as a permanent reside.

Intercessory—[in-ter-ses-*uh*-ree] To act or interpose in behalf of someone in difficulty or trouble, as by pleading or petition.

Intertwined—[ɪn tərˈtwaɪn] To twine together.

Insane—Not sane; not of sound mind; mentally deranged.

Itinerant—[ahy-tin-er-*uh* nt, ih-tin-] A person who travels from place to place, especially for duty or business.

J

Justification—A reason, fact, circumstance, or explanation that justifies or defends.

K

Kaffirs—The word is derived from the Arabic term kafir (meaning 'disbeliever'), which originally had the meaning 'one without religion.

L

Lamentations—[lam-*uh* n-tey-sh*uh* n] The book of the Bible in the OT.

Landlocked—Shut in completely, or almost completely by land.

Latin—An Italic language spoken in ancient Rome.

Langur (the golden)—An Old World monkey found in a small region of western Assam, India and in the neighboring foothills of the Black Mountains of Bhutan.

Legalism—Strict adherence, or the principle of strict adherence, to law or prescription

Leviticus—[lɪˈvɪt ɪ kəs] The third book of the Bible, containing laws relating to the priests and Levites and to the forms of Jewish ceremonial observance.

Licentiousness—[/laɪˈsɛn ʃəs/] Going beyond customary or proper bounds or limits; disregarding rules.

Linguistic—[/lɪŋˈgwɪs tɪk/] Of or belonging to language.

Lyres—[laɪər] A musical instrument of ancient Greece consisting of a sound box made typically from a turtle shell, with two curved arms connected by a yoke from which strings are stretched to the body, used especially to accompany singing and recitation.

M

Mammals—Any animal of the Mammalia, a large class of warm-blooded vertebrates having mammary glands in the female, a thoracic diaphragm, and a four-chambered heart. The class includes the whales, carnivores, rodents, bats.

Manual—Done, operated, worked, etc., by the hand or hands.

Maxims—A principle or rule of conduct.

Metaphor—A figure of speech in which a term or phrase is applied to something to which it is not literally applicable in order to suggest a resemblance.

Meticulous—[mə ˈtɪk yə ləs] Taking or showing extreme care about minute details; precise; thorough.

Merchant—[mɜr tʃənt] A person who buys and sells commodities for profit; dealer trader.

Microcredit—The lending of very small amounts of money at low interest, especially to a start-up company or self-employed person.

Monarchy—[mon-er-kee] A state or nation in which the supreme power is actually or nominally lodged in a monarch.

Monotonous—[m*uh*-not-n-*uh* s] Characterizing a sound continuing on one note.

Morality—Conformity to the rules of right conduct; moral or virtuous conduct.

Mozart—Austrian composer (1756–91)

Mundane—Common; ordinary; banal; unimaginative.

Multitude—A great number of people gathered together; crowd.

N

Narrative—[nær ə tɪv] A story or account of events, experiences, or the like, whether true or fictitious.

Nebuchadnezzar—[neb-*uh*-k*uh* d-nez-er, neb-yoo-] A king of Babylonia.

Nutritional—The act or process of nourishing or of being nourished.

O

Obscured—[*uh* b-skyoo r] Not clear to the understanding; hard to perceive.

Odor—The property of a substance that activates the sense of smell.

Oracle—[awr-*uh*-k*uh* l] The agency or medium giving such responses.

Origami—[awr-i-gah-mee] The traditional Japanese art or technique of folding paper into a variety or decorative or representational forms, as of animals or flowers.

p

Pagan—One of a people or community observing a polytheistic religion, as the ancient Romans and Greeks. (No longer in technical use.)

Papyrus—[p*uh*-pahy-r*uh* s] A material on which to write, prepared from thin strips of the pith of this plant laid together, soaked, pressed, and dried, used by the ancient Egyptians, Greeks, and Romans.

Parables—A statement or comment that conveys a meaning indirectly by the use of comparison, analogy, or the like.

Permissive—[per-mis-iv] Habitually or characteristically accepting or tolerant of something, as social behavior orlinguistic usage, that others might disapprove orforbid.

Perplexity—[pər ˈplɛk sɪ ti] A tangled, involved, or confused condition or situation.

Persistent—[per-sis-t*uh* nt] constantly repeated; continued.

Perspectives—[per-spek-tiv] A technique of depicting volumes and spatial relationships on a flat surface.

Persuaded—[per-sweyd] To prevail on (a person) to do something, as by advising or urging.

Piranhas—Any of several small South American freshwater fishes of the genus Serrasalmus that eat other fish and sometimes plants but occasionally also attack humans and other large animals that enter the water.

Phosphate—[fɒs feɪt] A carbonated drink of water and fruit syrup containing a little phosphoric acid.

Physiologist—[fiz-ee-ol-*uh*-jist] the branch of biology dealing with the functional and activities of living organisms and their parts including all physical and chemical processes

Plague—An epidemic disease that causes high mortality, pestilence.

Plunge—To cast or thrust forcibly or suddenly into something, as a liquid, a penetrable substance, a place, etc.; immerse; submerge.

Polyglot—Knowing or speaking different languages.

Polytheistic—The doctrine that there is more than one god or many gods.

Populous—[pop-*yuh*-luh s] Full of residents or inhabitants, as a region; heavily populated.

Principalities—The position or authority of a prince or chief ruler, sovereignty; supreme power.

Predominantly—Having ascendancy, power, authority, or influence over others; preeminent.

Preeminence—Eminent above or before others; superior; surpassing.

Protestant—Any Western Christian who is not an adherent of a Catholic, Anglican, or Eastern Church.

Punitive—[pyoo-ni-tiv] Serving for, concerned with, or inflicting punishment.

R

Radiolucent—[rey-dee-oh-loo-*suh* nt] almost transparent to electromagnetic radiation, esp X-rays.

Rapture—The carrying of a person to another place or sphere of existence.

Rectangular—Having one or more right angles.

Redemption—Theology. deliverance from sin; salvation.

Remonstrance—[ri-mon-str*uh* ns] To say or plead in protest, objection, or disapproval.

Renaissance—[ren-*uh*-sahns] The activity, spirit, or time of the great revival of art, literature, and learning in Europe beginning in the 14th century and extending to the 17th century.

Resumption—[ri-*zuh*mp-sh*uh* n] To go on or continue after interruption.

Revitalizing—[ree-vahyt-l-ahyz] To give new life to.

Riddles—A puzzling question, problem, or matter.

S

Sacredness—Devoted or dedicated to a deity or to some religious purpose; consecrated.

Sane—Having a sound, healthy mind.

Sanskrit—[san-skrit] An Indo European, Indic language, in use since c. 1200 b.c. as the religious and classical literary language of India.

Scrolls—A roll of parchment, paper, copper, or other material, especially one with writing on it: roll of parchment, paper, copper, or other material, especially one with writing on it.

Significant—[sig-nif-i-k*uh* nt] Important; of consequence.

Smeared—To spread or daub an oily, greasy, viscous, or wet substance on.

Sovereign—[sov-rin, sov-er-in, *suh*v-] A person who has supreme power or authority.

Sovereignty—The status, dominion, power, or authority of a sovereign.

Species—A class of individuals having some common characteristics or qualities.

Strand—To leave helpless, as without transport or money, etc

Strenuous—[stren-yoo-*uh* s] Requiring or involving the use of great energy or effort.

Subsequent—[*suh*b-si-kw*uh* nt] Occurring or coming later or after.

Successor—A person or thing that follows, esp a person whosucceeds another in an office.

Superlative—The highest kind, quality, or order; surpassing allelse or others; supreme; extreme.

Sushi—A type of food preparation originating in Japan, consisting of cooked vinegared rice combined with other ingredients such as raw seafood, vegetables and sometimes tropical fruits.

Sutures—[soocher] A joining of the lips or edges of a wound or the like by stitching or some similar process.

Sworn—Having taken an oath.

Synagogues—[sin-*uh*-gog,-gawg] A Jewish house of worship, often having facilities for religious instruction.

Synoptic—[si-nop-tik] Of the 4 Gospels presenting the narrative of Christ's life and ministry.

Synopsis—[si-nop-sis] A brief summary of the plot of a novel, motion picture, play, etc.

T

Theocracy—[thee-ok-*ruh*-see] A form of government in which God or a deity is recognized as the supreme civil ruler.

Theocratic— [thee-*uh*-krat-ik] The Rule of God which serves as a supreme law.

Theological—[thee-*uh*-loj-i-k*uh* l] Based upon the nature and will of God as revealed to humans.

Transfiguration—[trans-fig-y*uh*-rey-sh*uh* n] To change so as to glorify or exalt.

Transgression—[trans-gresh-*uh* n, tranz-] To break or breach of a law, etc; sin or crime.

Treachery—[trech-*uh*-ree] violation of faith; betrayal of trust.

Truisms—A self-evident, obvious truth.

Tychicus—[tɪtʃɪkəs/] Accompanied the Apostle Paul on a part of his missionary journey.

U

UAE—United Arab Emirates, and its capital is Abu Dhabi.

Unheeded—Disregard, ignore.

V

Vindicated—[vin-di-keyt] To clear, as from an accusation, imputation,suspicion, or the like.

W

Wanderings—Moving from place to place without a fixed plan;

Wages—Earnings, emolument, compensation,

Wrought—[rawt] Not rough or crude.

Y

Ylang-ylang—[ee-lahng-ee-lahng] An aromatic tree, Cananga odorata, of the annona family, native to the Philippines, Java, etc, having fragrant, drooping flowers that yield a volatile oil used in perfumery.

Z

Zephaniah—[zef-*uh*-nahy-*uh*] A book of the Bible bearing his name.

Zoroastrians—One of the world's oldest monotheistic religions emerged from a common prehistoric Indo-Iranian religious system dating to the early 2nd BC.

References

www.mapsofworld.com

www.gotquestions.org/Book

www.wikipedia.org

www.cia.gov/library/publications/the-world-factbook

www.biblegateway.com

CPSIA information can be obtained
at www.ICGtesting.com
Printed in the USA
BVHW050722260321
603213BV00003B/6